THE DIOCESAN CHANCELLOR

AN HISTORICAL SYNOPSIS
AND COMMENTARY

THE CATHOLIC UNIVERSITY OF AMERICA
CANON LAW STUDIES
No. 167

The Diocesan Chancellor

AN HISTORICAL SYNOPSIS AND COMMENTARY

BY

REV. JOHN EDWARD PRINCE, A.B., J.C.L.
Priest of the Diocese of Spokane

A DISSERTATION

Submitted to the Faculty of Canon Law of the Catholic University of America in Partial Fulfillment of the Requirements for the Degree of Doctor of Canon Law

THE CATHOLIC UNIVERSITY OF AMERICA PRESS
WASHINGTON, D. C.
1942

NIHIL OBSTAT:

EDUARDUS ROELKER, S.T.D., J.C.D.
Censor Deputatus
Washingtonii, die XI Maii, 1942.

IMPRIMATUR:

✠CAROLUS D. WHITE, D.D.
Episcopus Spokanensis
Spokanii, die XI Maii, 1942.

MURRAY & HEISTER
WASHINGTON, D. C.

PRINTED BY

TIMES AND NEWS PUBLISHING CO.
GETTYSBURG, PA., U. S. A.

TO MY FATHER

and to the memory of

MY MOTHER

TABLE OF CONTENTS

CANONICAL COMMENTARY

FOREWORD

This is a study of the office of diocesan chancellor as it is found in the general law. In many dioceses of the United States the chancellor has become a personage of distinction, influence, power and administrative responsibility. This dignity has given to the office of chancellor a unique position in this country not found in the practice of the universal Church or in the provisions of the law. There will be some discussion in this work about the particular functions exercised by the chancellor in the United States, but the main purpose of the present study is to investigate the historical development and to furnish a commentary on the legal office of diocesan chancellor as defined by the Code of Canon Law.

In the historical part it is not intended to give an exhaustive treatment of the various offices of chancellors in their history and development. To do so would necessitate a long research through the records of numerous archives of ancient European dioceses from their earliest beginnings, which is neither practical nor necessary to gain a general view of the historical development of the office. The growth of the organization of the episcopal chancery or curia is not directly within the scope of this treatment, or the development of the offices of Royal or Papal or University chancellors through the centuries. Only the historical development of those functions which are included in the concept of the office of diocesan chancellor as found in the present Code will be the subject of this investigation.

The second part of this work will be a commentary on the legal provision regarding the office of diocesan chancellor as found in canon 372. It will contain a description of the office and furnish an explanation of its double function. It will consider the qualities necessary in a chancellor and thereupon will discuss the powers which may be delegated to him. In particular, the practice of employing the chancellor as a general delegate will be considered at length.

The author takes occasion to express his gratitude to His Excellency, the Most Reverend Charles D. White, Bishop of Spokane, for the opportunity to pursue advanced studies. He is also genuinely thankful for the guidance given him by the members of the Faculty of the School of Canon Law at the Catholic University of America.

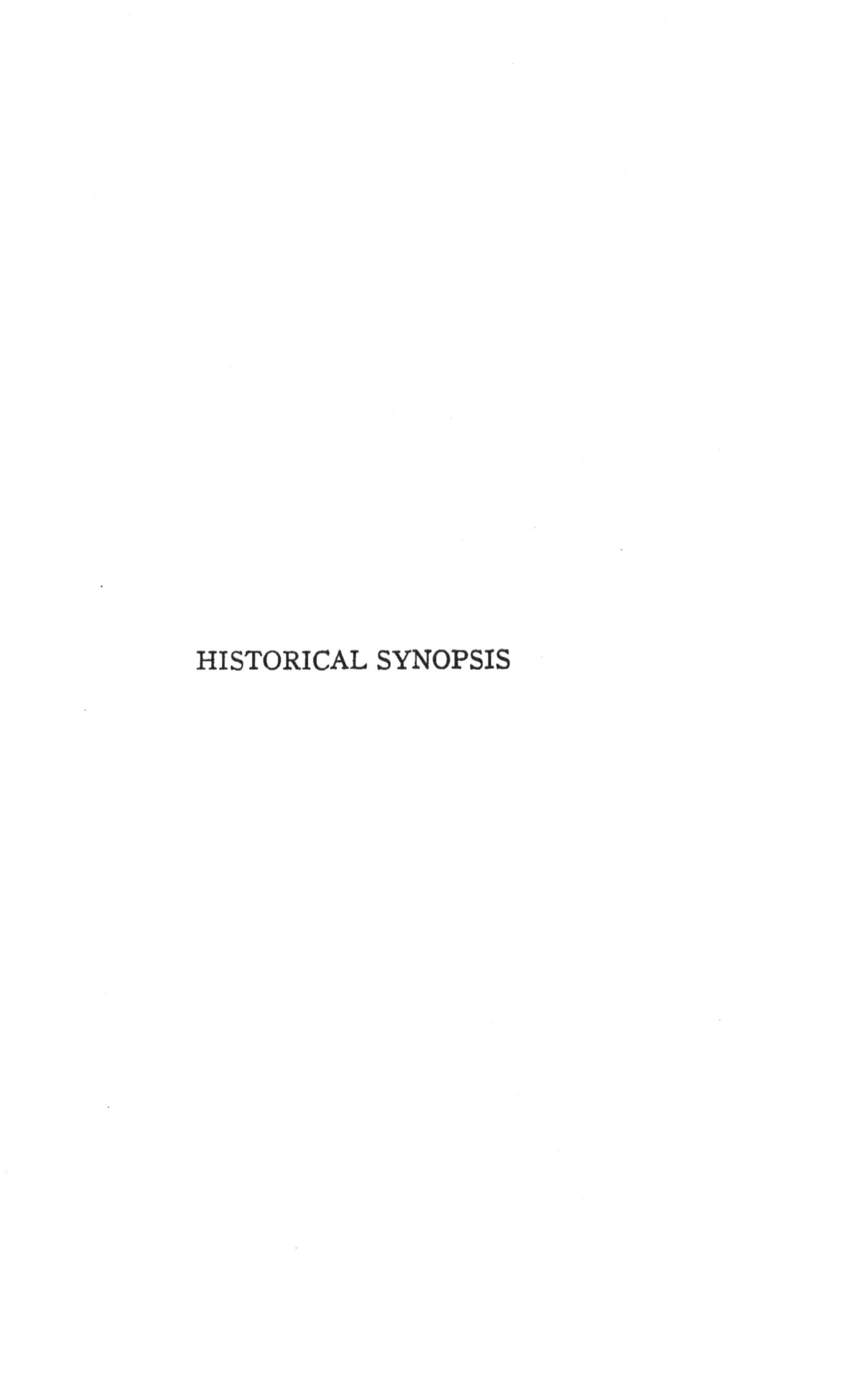

HISTORICAL SYNOPSIS

CHAPTER I

Preliminary Notions

The derivation of the word *chancellor* can be traced to the Latin word *cancer*.[1] Because the *cancer* (crab) moved itself crosswise, leaving marks in the sand somewhat in the manner of an "X" as it travelled, the word *cancer* came to mean a similar crossing of lines, bars or sticks. When the limits of a field or of some definite place were set off by binding many sticks together in a transverse fashion, they were called *cancelli* (diminutive of *cancer*) or a lattice-work.[2] In ancient Rome the term *cancellarius* came to be commonly used as the name for the *ostiarius* or door-keeper who stood at the lattice-work or bar which separated the magistrate in the Roman law courts from the people. It had previously been employed as a name for the officer who read the notices of the Emperor to the people from the *cancelli* or lattice-work of the casements of the palace.[3]

The duty of the *cancellarius* or chancellor who stood at the bar of justice was to admit petitioners to the magis-

[1] Lexicographers quote Sextus Pompeius Festus, a grammarian of about the year 300.

[2] Moerner, *Dissertatio academica de cancellariis* (Upsaliae, 1790), p. 3.

[3] Cf. Du Cange, *Glossarium ad scriptores latinitatis* (6 vols., Parisiis, 1733), II, 130; Moroni, *Dizionario di Erudizione Storico Ecclesiastica* (103 vols., Venezia, 1840-1861), VII, 154; Forcellini, *Lexicon totius latinitatis* (Pataviae, 1871), v. "cancellarius." An interesting letter describing the *cancellarius* as he functioned in the Roman court is found in Cassiodorus, *II variarum, ep. 6—Monumenta Germaniae Historica, Auctores Antiquissimi*, Tom. XII (ed. Mommsen, Berolini: apud Weidmannos, 1894), 135. (Hereafter cited as *MGH*.)

trate, and he gradually came to do the work of a secretary in the writing of the documents necessary for the court.[4]

When there was need for erasures in documents, this was sometimes done by forming over the words to be deleted a series of crossed lines (*cancelli*). The performance of this act was designated with the word *cancellare,* and probably the one who crossed out the words was called *cancellarius.*[5] Ferraris gives two interesting verses from a preface of a book of Polycarp which bring out this use of the word *cancellare*:—

"Hic est, qui leges regni cancellat iniquas,
Et mandata pii principis aequa facit."[6]

The word *cancellare* was also used for expressing the action of crossing the arms in prayer as well as the action of stretching the hands by joining them together and crossing the fingers.[7]

In Roman Law the office of chancellor was purely a secular one.[8] It was taken over by the barbarian kings

---

[4] Cassiodorus, *loc. cit.*—*MGH, loc. cit.*, Savigny, *The History of Roman Law during the Middle Ages* (translated by Cathcart, Edinburgh, 1859), p. 53. (This work is hereafter referred to as Savigny-Cathcart.)

[5] Ferraris, *Prompta bibliotheca canonica, iuridica, moralis, theologica necnon ascetica, polemica, historica* (9 vols., Romae, 1885-1899), II, 38-42; Chokier, *Commentaria in regulas cancellariae apostolicae* (3 ed., Coloniae Agrippae, 1674), p. 14.

[6] *Prompta bibliotheca,* II, 38, footnote.

[7] Moerner, *Dissertatio academica de cancellariis,* pp. 3, 4.

[8] Cf. Seeck, "Cancellarius"—Pauly-Wissowa, *Real-Encyclopaedie der classischen Altertumswissenschaft,* III (Stuttgart, 1899), 1456-1459; Mommsen, *Gesammelte Schriften* (6 vols., Berlin, 1910), VI, 417; The Emperor Justinian (527-565) speaks of chancellors a few times in his law, but only in a civil sense; they had no function in the Church: e.g.: "Consiliarios judicum et cancellarios . . . in provinciis residere praecipimus"—C. (1, 51) 3; "Nullus judicum . . . secum ducere audeat, cui domestici vel cancellarii nomen imponat . . ."—C. (1, 51) 8; "Nemo in provinciis, qui semel domestici vel cancellarii ministerium gesserit."—C. (1, 51) 5.

at the breakup of the Roman Empire and became an office of great dignity by virtue of the fact that the royal chancellor was keeper of the king's seal.[9]

However this treatise does not deal with the royal chancellors or the Papal chancellors, but is limited solely to the diocesan chancellor as defined in the present Code of Canon Law;[10] he is a priest whose principal work is to care for the curial archives, and who is by his very office a notary. By *notary* is here understood a public person who, by his subscription, certifies a document.[11] The function of the notary has been employed by the Church from its very beginning for the duties of writing documents,[12] but notaries as such do not come directly within the scope of this treatment. Only that office that has in it the characteristic function of a notary-archivist, as the office of chancellor outlined in the present law, will be dealt with.

It is the purpose of the historical part of this dis-

---

[9] Murray, *A New English Dictionary on historical principles* (Oxford, 1893), II, 264. The history of the European kingdoms is replete with many examples of the power of the royal chancellor which can be found in any textbook treating of medieval history: cf. Bresslau, *Handbuch der Urkundenlehre für Deutschland und Italien* (2. ed., 2 vols., Leipzig, 1912), I, 441-583 (This work is hereafter cited as Bresslau, *Handbuch*); cf. also Thomassinus, *Vetus et Nova Ecclesiae disciplina circa beneficia et beneficiarios* (3 vols., Mogontiaci, 1787), pars I, lib. II, capp. CV-CVI (This work is cited as Thomassinus in the following references to it).

[10] "In qualibet curia constituatur ab Episcopo cancellarius qui sit sacerdos, cuius praecipuum munus sit acta curiae in archivo custodire, ordine chronologico disponere et de eisdem indicis tabulam conficere . . . cancellarius est eo ipso notarius"—Can. 372.

[11] Can. 373, § 1.

[12] The earliest Church notaries in Rome wrote the acts of the martyrs; e.g., "Anteros . . . martyrio coronatur . . . hic gestas martyrum diligenter a notariis equisivit et in ecclesia recondit . . . Fabianus efficit VII subdiaconos qui VII notariis immineret ut gestas martyrum integre fideliter colligerent"—Duchesne, *Liber Pontificalis* (Parisiis, 1866), I, 147-148.

sertation to trace the development leading up to the present-day legislation on the office of the chancellor. To do this, an investigation is made into both the practice and the laws that have preceded the present Code of Canon Law and that have dealt with the *idea* of the chancellor of the diocese as it existed, even when this conception of the office may not have been expressed by the term chancellor. An investigation into both law *and* practice is made, because before the sixteenth century there is practically no ecclesiastical legislation, even of a particular nature, which provided for this office of diocesan chancellor. A search of the sources available to the writer reveals that in no place up to the sixteenth century were there any precise ecclesiastical laws with regard to this office as it is now mentioned and defined in the Code. In fact there existed no *general* law which defined the office of diocesan chancellor before the present Code.

That the chancellor was a notary by ecclesiastical authority is established in the practice of the thirteenth century; that he was a custodian of archives at the same time in his capacity of curial notary is a development that becomes established through particular legislation in Italy in the sixteenth century.

CHAPTER II

Historical Development Before the Sixteenth Century

ARTICLE 1. EARLY EVIDENCES

During the first three centuries when bishops were the only pastors in the dioceses[13] there is no evidence of the present-day idea of the chancellor of the diocese. The only archives of the bishops of this period were the *diptichs* or records of baptism which the bishop kept in his own house.[14]

There can be found in Roman Law evidences of the separate functions of offices to which attached the care of documents as well as the duty of acting as notary. Thus the idea of chancellor is there, although it seems to exist chiefly with relation to a civil capacity. There is the *tabellio,* who is referred to quite often when mention is made of the drawing up of public documents such as contracts and wills.[15] Savigny claims that these *tabelliones,* who were sometimes called chancellors and who wrote these public documents, were not constituted by public authority.[16] Fournier claims for them a certain public authority in that they put their signature to public instruments which they themselves drew up.[17]

---

[13] Thomassinus, pars I, lib. II, cap. XXI, n. 4.

[14] Catalanus, *Rituale Romanum Benedicti XIV,* I,32: II,344, in O'Rourke, *Parish Registers* (Washington: Catholic University of America Press, 1934), p. 31.

[15] C. Th. (1, 12); C. (1, 2) 14, 3.

[16] Savigny-Cathcart, p. 53.

[17] Fournier, *Les officialités au moyen age* (Paris, 1880), chapt. VI, "des notaires," p. 41.

And again in Roman Law Justinian (527-565) ordered that the archives in all the provinces be kept in special buildings to be erected for them,[18] and in Constantinople he designated ecclesiastical *chartularii* or keepers of archives and made rules for them.[19] These last named were something like the chancellor of the present day legislation in that they prepared a catalogue of the archives and subscribed their signature to them. This same Emperor mentions also *actuarii, scrinarii* and *exceptori* who in varying manner perform functions that are done by the diocesan chancellor according to the present practice. But these officials in their various functions show only the existence of the "idea," and not the exact office of the present diocesan chancellor. Theirs were entirely civil functions.[20]

An investigation of the practice of the important Church of Constantinople reveals the existence of an ecclesiastical office that had some of the functions similar to those the present law gives to the office of chancellor. This was the office of the *cartophylax*. The cleric in this office acted as archivist and testified to the authenticity of documents under his care. However, this was but a small part of his work, for he had many powers which today belong to the *officialis* and the vicar general.[21]

As early as the year 343 a decree of the Council of Sardica mentioned the archives of the Church of Constantinople,[22] and in the year 475 they are mentioned by

---

[18] N. (15, 5) 2.

[19] C. (1, 2) 25; N. (74, 4) 2.

[20] C. (12, 49).

[21] Cf. Boudinhon, "Cartophylax,"—*Le canoniste contemporain,* XIX (1896), 366.

[22] Harduin, *Acta conciliorum et epistolae decretales ac constitutiones summorum pontificum* (12 vols., Parisiis, 1715), I, 672. This collectioı will be hereinafter cited as Harduin.

Arcadius of Constantinople in writing to Pope St. Simplicius.[23] At the sixth ecumenical council, held at Constantinople in 680, a *cartophylax* is mentioned among the members of the secretariate of the Patriarch of Constantinople as archivist, and at the same time there are named two chancellors and a notary.[24]

In the Council of Constantinople which was held in the year 870 there is mentioned Anastasius, the *cartophylax* (who is also called *bibliothecarius*), who was the custodian of the archives and had great power and dignity because of this office.[25] In successive councils the *cartophylax,* whose office was by that time coupled with that of the archdeacon and seems to have provided for an intermediary between the clerics and the patriarch,[26] is seen to have the function of confirming, or of sealing and subscribing the charts,[27] and also the duty of witnessing professions of faith and of signing letters.[28] And thus it appears that the *cartophylax* of the Greek Church, among the other functions of his office, had also the duty of caring for the archives, as well as the function of a notary.

In the African Church there are also indications of

---

[23] Harduin, II, 805.

[24] Act 8: "Quidam ex secretario . . . sanctissime patriarchae constantinopoleos, i.e., Georgius diaconus et Cartophylax, Anastasius diaconus et notarius et defensor navium . . . Stephanus diaconus et cancellarius . . ." —Mansi, *Sacrorum conciliorum nova et amplissima collectio* (53 vols. in 59, Paris, Arnhem, Leipzig, 1901-1927), XI, 801. Hereafter this collection will be cited as Mansi. Cf. also acts 12, 13, 14 of this same council.

[25] *Adnotationes Anastasii bibliothecarii ad synodum VIII* (IV Const. [870]),—Harduin, V, 942.

[26] Cf. Boudinhon, "Cartophylax,"—*Le canoniste contemporain,* XIX (1896), 366.

[27] Council of Constantinople (1166),—Mansi, XXII, 14.

[28] Council of Nymphaeum in Bithynia (1234),—Mansi, XXIII, 299, 319.

the existence of an office of archivist. The Council of Mileve (402), for instance, decided that a register of the dates of the consecration of bishops was to be preserved in the archives of the Numidian Church.[29] Then again in 525 Boniface of Carthage mentions the archives of that Church on at least three different occasions.[30] Another indication of the existence of an archivist-notary is found in the order of Caesarius, Bishop of Arles (502-542), demanding that authentic documents be made of the proceedings of the II Council of Orange (529) and that they be kept in the archives of the Bishop of Arles.[31] In the same century (about the year 575) a notary belonging to the principal church of Ravenna had the care of some of the documents made by the other notaries of that city.[32]

ARTICLE 2. THE MIDDLE AGES

After the breaking up of the Roman Empire the barbarian kings took over into their own courts the civil office of chancellor. This can be seen in the legislation added to the traditionary barbarian laws. This legislation provided that the office of chancellor should continue to answer to the functions requisite in the preparation and care of charts (*cartae*).[33] In Carolingian

[29] Canon 86—Mansi, III, 786.

[30] Harduin, II, 1074, 1077, and 1084.

[31] *MGH, Legum Sectio III, Concilia aevi merovingici*, Tom.I (ed. Fredericus Maassen, Hannoverae, 1893), 53; Mansi, VIII, 712.

[32] *Marini papiri*, n. 74, col. 8, lin. 1—a manuscript quoted in Savigny-Cathcart, chap. V, p. 6.

[33] *MGH, Leges* (5 toms., toms. I, II, III, and IV, ed. Georgius Pertz, Hannoverae, 1835-1868, tom. V, ed. Societas aperiendis fontibus rerum germanicarum medii aevi, Hannoverae, 1899), IV, 524, and V, 248. (This is hereinafter cited as *MGH, Leges.*)

times this civil chancellor was vested with public authority to affirm the authenticity of *cartae*,[34] and there are indications that he may have functioned also as a judge in some minor cases.[35]

Bresslau says that in Merovingian times there are references to civil notaries who are at times called chancellors who were generally clerics employed as scribes. But by the end of the eighth century they themselves, though subscribing their names as chancellors to the completed documents, in turn employed other scribes to do the actual writing. He cites sources.[36] The interchanging of the terms "notary" and "chancellor" for the one who acted as a scribe was quite common. Even as early as the ninth century an example of this is found in the legislation of King Lothaire.[37] In the year 803 Charlemagne made the notary-chancellors civil public persons and established them in every province.[38]

---

[34] "Si vero testes defuerint, cum duabus cartis, qui eiusdem cancellarii manu firmatae sint vel subscriptae, cuiuscumque fuerint, suam cartam, quae tertia est, veracem et legitimam esse confirmet," *Caroli Magni capitula minora a. 803*, cap. "de innuitate cartarum"—*MGH, Leges*, I, 116; ". . . cancellarii . . . suam cartam firment," *Liber papiensis ludovici pii*, n. 5—*MGH, Leges*, IV, 524; "Ut cancellarii veraces cartas publice conscribant . . . scripta carta . . . verax agnoscatur," *Liber papiensis lotharii*, n. 12—*MGH, Leges*, IV, 542.

[35] "Ut nullus cancellarius pro ullo judicato aut scripto aliud amplius accipere audeat," *Capitularia Lotharii I*, cap. 13—*MGH, Legum Sectio II, Capitularia regum francorum* (2 toms., ed. Alfredus Boretius et Victor Krause, Hannoverae, tom. I, 1890, tom. II, 1897), I, 62. (This is hereinafter cited as *MGH, Legum Sectio II*).

[36] Bresslau, *Handbuch*, I, 592-593.

[37] In the same law the chancellor and the notary are mentioned in regard to their writings; first that the chancellor should only receive a certain remuneration for his writings, and secondly that the notary should swear that he has written nothing untrue. See *liber papiensis lotharii*, n. 71—*MGH, Leges*, IV, 552.

[38] *MGH, Leges*, I, 116.

This was an important law for it was the first time that chancellors were given the legal authority to be official public notaries in all the provinces of the Empire. Two years later, in 805, Charlemagne gave every bishop the civil power to establish his own notary public, distinct from the ordinary scribes of the bishop, and by the very act of appointment by the bishop he was to be recognized as a public person by the king.[39] This, too, was an important law for it furnishes the first definite evidence of the bishop, by his own authority, establishing a notary.[40] Though this legislation reflects a development in the office of notary-chancellor, yet this function cannot be called the office of chancellor as in the diocese of the present day, because at that early time there was no law to show that it involved anything more than a merely civil function.

This power of the bishop to institute public notaries, as recognized by the royal authorities, disappeared for two centuries after the Carolingian reform, and only the notaries appointed by the royal authority itself were officially recognized. However, in practice, other notaries than those of royal authority were *de facto* accepted. This came about from the fact that the clerics, who more generally than others could write, would draw up for the people private documents which came to be accepted as authentic. In this way clerics prac-

---

[39] *Capitulare duplex in thronis villa promulgatum,* n. 3—*MGH, Leges,* I, 131.

[40] At this time of the restoration of the episcopate there was also a tendency to give to every bishop a public notary who was also called a chancellor and was a civil officer to help the bishop administer his civil jurisdiction. Cf. Mangisch, *De la situation et de l'organization du notariat en Valais* (Saint-Maurice, 1913), pp. 23-30).

tically carried on the Carolingian tradition in the same manner as if they had been officially established by the bishop.[41] From the surveys made of catalogues of the acts of the churches it appears that no organized chancery of the bishop existed before the twelfth century,[42] and since clerics were the only ones who as a group were able to write, this explains why the notary tradition was carried on by clerics in writing out certain instruments, such as wills or contracts, in those places where a royal notary was not at hand.[43] That priests at this time often functioned in the office of civil notary-chancellor is seen from the prohibition of some of the local councils against this. Thus in France a council in the year 813 forbade priests to exercise the office of public chancellor.[44]

Throughout the remainder of the ninth century various indications seem to show that the concept of the office of chancellor included the function of notarizing and caring for documents. The famous Hincmar, Archbishop of Rheims (845-882), tells us that the duty of the civil chancellor had to do with writing and caring for the royal precepts and secret documents[45] although in another place he speaks of his diocesan archives that are so well kept by his *scrinarius,* without mentioning the chancellor in connection with the diocesan archives.[46]

---

[41] Böuard, *Manuel de diplomatique francaise et pontificale* (Paris, 1929), pp. 116-117. (Hereafter cited as Böuard, *Manuel*); Bresslau, *Handbuch,* I, 593-594; cf. Thomassinus, pars I, lib. II, cap. CVI, n. 3.

[42] Böuard, *Manuel,* pp. 114-115.

[43] Cf. Bresslau, *Handbuch,* I, 593; Böuard, *Manuel,* p. 116.

[44] II Council of Châlons, canon 44—Harduin, IV, 1039; Mansi, XIV, 102.

[45] ". . . cancellarius, qui a secretis olim appellabatur . . . qui praecepta regia . . . scriberent et secreta . . . custodirent," *De ordine palatii,* cap. 16—*MGH, Legum Sectio II,* II, 520.

[46] *Dissertatio secunda de praedestinatione,* cap. XXXVI—*MPL,* CXXV, 391.

This indicates that, although the idea of notary-archivist stands connected with the concept of the chancellor at this time, it is not yet that of the diocesan chancellor of our present day law. Again, among the articles drawn up in a Capitulary held at Aisne in 853 there is mention made of the *custom* existing at that time that the chancellor had care of the writings;[47] and in the year 888 a chancellor acted as notary in witnessing a royal pact between King Berengarius and the Venetians.[48]

In other references of this time there is the same idea of the chancellor as a notary and keeper of documents, yet no definite practice evidences an office such as the present one of diocesan chancellor.[49] This condition is more clearly understood when one realizes the fact that there was not as yet any such organization as our diocesan curia.[50] This seems to be the view of Savigny when he says that it is believed that the curial system found in the Theodosian Code (1, 12) continued up to the beginning of the twelfth century.[51] For it wasn't till the twelfth century that the diocesan curia became really organized under the direction of the bishop.

The same clerics who were able to write and were helping the people in drawing up their private documents were at the same time employed by the bishop in preparing and keeping his documents, whether of ecclesiastical or civil administration, and they were variously and

---

[47] Cap. 11,—*MGH, Legum sectio II*, II, 274.

[48] Pactum Berengarii I,—*MGH, Legum sectio II*, I, 145.

[49] Many references to chancellors of this time are given in the diplomatic manuals. Cf. for example, Giry, *Manuel de diplomatique* (Paris, 1894), p. 808.

[50] Cf. Böuard, *Manuel*, p. 114; Giry, *Manuel*, p. 814.

[51] Savigny-Cathcart, *op. cit.*, p. 303.

sometimes indiscriminately termed "chancellor," "notary" or simply "secretary."

ARTICLE 3. FORMATIVE PERIOD OF THE DIOCESAN CURIA

The idea of a bishop's curia began to develop with the feudal system of the tenth and eleventh centuries. The counts and the bishops of this time had in their castles a quasi-curia modelled after the royal chancellery. This can be seen from an examination and comparison of the charts in the archives of the various ancient European churches.[53] The chaplain was often the one who drew up the documents and especially the ecclesiastical acts of these quasi-curias of the castles; and he was often called chancellor after the fashion of the royal chancellors. It was the royal chancellor who prepared and sealed the official documents of the king. This all was an example to be followed in the bishop's chancery which began to take form in the twelfth century.[54] However, this is not an indication that these chancellor-notaries of the counts and bishops were public persons in that they were officially constituted to authenticate documents by authority of the bishop as was the case under Charlemagne's provision of the year 805. Both Bresslau[55] and Böuard[56] say that the institution of public

[52] Bresslau (*Handbuch,* I, 590-601) gives many references from German dioceses or individual churches up to the eleventh century. These references furnish examples showing how these various officers drew up or helped in the preparing of the documents of these churches.

[53] Böuard, *Manuel,* pp. 115-117, contains citations of sources dealing with the charts of this period in the archives of old churches.

[54] Cf. Böuard, *Manuel,* pp. 116, 117; Giry, *Manuel,* p. 809.

[55] *Handbuch,* I, 593-594.

[56] *Op. cit.,* pp. 40-43, 115.

persons appointed by the authority of the bishop did not take place any more after the Carolingian reform until the twelfth century. The only public notaries who were authorized to act officially at this time were those who were established by the royal authority. The chancery conditions were not very good at this time, and even though episcopal documents were signed by those who called themselves notaries of the bishop,[57] these were not necessarily ecclesiastic notaries in the strict sense of a *public person* officially accredited by the bishop. The distinction between an ecclesiastic notary who could authenticate a public document and simply a notary who wrote documents was not very clear.[58]

But now in the twelfth century the organization of a formal bishop's chancellery takes definite form principally through the chapter of the cathedral church. For instance, at this time in Sion, an important city on the Rhone in Switzerland, the bishop started a chancellery by giving the functions of the office of chancellor as known in the royal courts (*per ipsum cancellarium conficiuntur omnia instrumenta*) to a member of the collegiate group of the cathedral chapter.[59] Böuard speaks of a renaissance "romano-canonique," deriving from Italy, which at this time introduced the idea of a public notariate into France.[60] And Fournier says that the chancellor was an officer attached to the cathedral chapter and who cared for the seal (*sceau*) of the

[57] E.g., the Council of Rheims (1050), canon 7, classes a notary among the officials of the bishop.—Mansi, XIX, 753.

[58] Giry, *Manuel*, p. 814.

[59] Mangisch, *De la situation et de l'organization du notariat en Valais*, p. 48.

[60] *Manuel*, p. 156.

church.[61] Although all the members of the cathedral chapter could act as notaries, it was only one member, who was generally the chaplain of the bishop, who acted in the chapter as a chancellor, that is, he was at the head of the whole documentary system with the other scribes under him, himself having the responsibility of caring for and signing the letters of the bishop.[62] This practice existed also in the Western Patriarchal See of Aquileia in northern Italy.[63] Moore gives to the chancellor of this time a two-fold function: he saw to the redaction of the official acts of the cathedral chapter of which he was a member, by sealing and delivering these acts; and his other duty was to take care of the needs of education in the diocese.[64]

From the end of the twelfth century the inferior chancelleries more and more imitated the royal chancellery, following the same formulas in their procedure as were employed in the Papal Chancellery. As these inferior diocesan chancelleries became more organized it was quite logical that they would model themselves, at least to some degree, upon those of the king and the Pope.[65] Just as there was a special officer of the king

---

[61] *Les officialités au moyen age,* p. xx. On page 43 he quotes written acts of the bishops of the twelfth century.

[62] Cf. Bresslau, *Handbuch,* I, 596, 597. He says here that from the year 1107 the chaplain of the Archbishop of Köln was the chancellor and head of the documentary system and quotes sources to show that this was also the practice in other dioceses (*"cancellaria nostra quae vulgo cappellaria vocantur"*).

[63] "Ego Chuonardus domini patriarchae cappellanus jussu ipsius, et petitione canonicorum Aquilegensis ecclesiae hanc paginam scripsi et dedi." Council of Aquileia (1181)—Mansi, XXII, 474.

[64] Moore, *The Works of Peter of Poitiers* (Washington, 1936), p. 12; cf. also Luchaire, *Social France at the time of Philip Augustus* (translated from the 2. ed. by Krehbiel, London, 1912), pp. 89, 124, 125.

[65] Cf. Böuard, *Manuel,* p. 155; Giry *Manuel,* p. 809.

who drew up and sealed the royal documents, and who was called the chancellor,[66] so also the officer who performed this same function for the bishop was often called the chancellor upon the formation of the bishop's chancellery. This name was generally applied to the one who was at the head of the whole documentary system of the diocese, and not to the ordinary notaries or scribes who worked under him.[67] This was the general practice at the end of the twelfth century. It is not till the next century that there is found a general ecclesiastical regulation providing for the establishment of a public ecclesiastical person in the diocese to authenticate documents.

ARTICLE 4. THE EFFECT OF THE EXPANSION OF EDUCATION ON THE OFFICE OF CHANCELLOR IN THE THIRTEENTH CENTURY

With the development of education in the thirteenth century a new function was exercised by the bishop's chancellor. He was charged with the duty of regulating the teaching and lecturing in the new universities that began to arise. This gradually became a new office which was later termed *Chancellor of the University;* but at this time the same person who had charge of the documentary system also regulated the courses of education. In fact, the first direct legislation that treats explicitly of the diocesan chancellor includes this function in the work of education.

[66] Examples of these royal chancellors acting in the preparation and care of documents can be found in Thomassinus, pars I, lib. II, cap. CVI; also in Mansi, XXII, 182, 184; cf. Morel, *La grande chancellerie royal et l'expedition des lettres royaux* (Paris, 1900), chap. I.

[67] Bresslau, *Handbuch,* I, 601.

The first ecclesiastical law about the office of diocesan chancellor is found in a constitution of the Diocese of Lincoln in England in 1212.[68] Here the office of diocesan chancellor is defined. He has the custody of the seal of the cathedral chapter, composes its letters and is in charge of the church books and records. His principal duties however seem to have had to do with the superintendence of schools, with the granting of permission to preach, and in general with those things that pertained to the task of teaching in the diocese.[69] In those dioceses of England where there were universities, the diocesan chancellor seems to have had full charge of them. This office later became a separate function of itself of great importance and dignity. It was no longer under the care of the chancellor of the diocese, but the person who occupied this position kept the name of chancellor and this nomenclature remains even to modern times in connection with the position of *Chancellor of the University.*[70] This same development took place in Paris, where the chancellor of the documentary system in the chapter cared for the regulation of teaching, and from this a new office arose which became that of the Chancellor of the University of Paris.[71]

[68] *Constitutiones Lincolnien. Ecclesiae, a. 1212,* "de officio cancellarii"—Wilkins, *Concilia Magnae Brittaniae et Hiberniae* (4 vols., Londini, 1737), I, 536.

[69] "Officium cancellarii est scholas regere, praedicare vel per se vel per alium . . . item libros legendarum corrigere . . . Dignitas ipsius est, quod nullus potest legere in civitate Lincoln. nisi de licentia ipsius, et quod omnes scholas in comitatu Lincoln. pro suo confert arbitrio."—Wilkins, *op. cit.,* I, 536.

[70] Du Cange, *Glossarium ad scriptores latinitatis* (6 vols., Parisiis, 1753), II, 143; Benson, *The Cathedral* (London: Murray, 1878), p. 32. Examples of this university chancellor in the English Church legislation can be found also in Wilkins, *op. cit.,* III, 166, 358.

[71] *Constitutiones Cardinalis Gallonis, a. 1208,* cap. IX—Mansi, XXIII, 765; Benson, *The Cathedral,* p. 53, and footnote.

In Germany, though there is not found the same office of university chancellor at that period, yet the same tendency of the use of the officer who cared for the chapter's documents as also the one for the work of superintending the schools is found. This person was sometimes called the *scholasticus* of the chapter. In addition to his other duties he had care of the books used in the schools and made changes in them. He was custodian of the seal of the church to which he was attached and acted as secretary of the chapter.[72]

This function of regulating the work of education in the diocese is no part of the present day legal office of the chancellor, and therefore its further development is not directly the concern of this treatise.

In the twelfth and thirteenth centuries there is not found any legally constituted office of diocesan chancellor whose function was that of archivist-notary of the diocese, despite indications that a person who was sometimes called *chancellor* performed one or the other or both of these functions together with other duties. It is sufficient for the purpose of this historical search to know that no legal office of diocesan chancellor, as defined in the present Code, existed at that time, even though there were indications of the idea of this office existing in practice, but with relation to different and varying functions in the diocese.

---

[72] "Item scholasticus erit custos minoris sigilli ecclesiae et omnes litteras capituli scribi faciat suis sumptibus et expensis, librosque scholasticos custodiens reformabit . . . ," *Statuta ecclesiae Schwerin., a. 1238—Schneider, Die Entwicklung der bishöflichen Domkapitel* (Mainz, 1882), p. 97, footnote.

ARTICLE 5. THE EFFECT OF THE NEED OF A NOTARY JUDICIAL PROCEDURE FROM THE THIRTEENTH CENTURY

As the chancelleries of the bishops began to develop, the judicial and extra-judicial procedure called for the repeated use of authentic documents and written testimony. This necessitated the employment of a notary who had ecclesiastical power to draw up documents in an authentic manner, so that they would be acceptable in the ecclesiastical forum. He should be able to subscribe to written testimony with such authority that it could be referred to in the future as authentic, even though the witnesses who had given the testimony were no longer present. Although such public persons existed already under civil authority, the Church during the first part of the thirteenth century enacted its first general legislation in regard to the establishment of a public person of ecclesiastical authority in the diocesan curia.[73] This is found in the legislation of Pope Innocent III (1198-1216) in canon 38 of the IV General Council of the Lateran (1215), in which the bishop is ordered to have a *public person* or two other competent men for the work of drawing up both judicial and extra-judicial acts. This law was later incorporated in the Gregorian Decretals.[74] This legislation seems to be the beginning of a movement to replace the variously termed notaries of the

---

[73] D'Angelo, *La Curia Diocesana* (Giarre, 1922), p. 28; Lega-Bartoccetti, *Commentarius in iudicia ecclesiastica* (3 vols., Romae, 1938-1941), I, 147, n. 3.

[74] ". . . ut tam in ordinario judicio quam extraordinario iudex semper adhibeat aut publicam si potest haberi personam, aut duos viros idoneos, qui fideliter universa iudicii acta exscribant . . ."—C. 11, X, *de probationibus*, II, 19; cf. Mansi, XXIII, 154.

former episcopal chanceries and cathedral chapters with judicial notaries.[75] These notaries, acting in the chancery in judicial and administrative procedure as public persons, went by various names such as *tabellio, notarius, actuarius* and *cancellarius,* and these terms were used interchangeably as they had often been employed when they had signified civil notaries. The common use of these various names for the same person is seen in certain decretal laws on the relation of public persons and clerics, and also in the comments on these laws by the decretalists.[76]

Since the decretals had forbidden clerics to act as public *tabelliones* or notaries, these decretalists discussed the question of whether these public persons in the ecclesiastical curia should be laymen or priests.[77] The fact was that both clerics and laymen acted in the capacity of episcopal notary and were termed *cancellarius* at times.[78] Wernz-Vidal say that to interpret title 50 of the third book of the decretals as forbidding clerics to act in the ecclesiastical curia as public persons is too strict and contrary to the custom of that time.[79]

From the decretal legislation[80] and the discussion of

---

[75] Cf. Fournier, *Les officialitès au moyen age,* p. 46.

[76] C. 8, X, *ne clerici vel monachi saecularibus negotiis se immisceant,* III, 50; C. 11, *de haereticis,* VI, 2, in VIo; cf. decretalists on Tit. 50, liber III, of the Decretals of Gregory IX: Henricus Hostiensis; Joannes Andreae; Augustinus Barbosa.

[77] Cf. Prosper Fagnanus, *Commentarium in decretalium libros* (Romae, 1661), lib. III, tit. 50, n. 56 sq.

[78] Cf. Caietanus, *Iuris canonici universi commentarius* (Monachii, 1703), lib. II, tit. XXII, cap. I, nn. 14-15.

[79] Wernz, F. X., et Vidal, Petrus, *Ius canonicum ad codicis normam exactum* (7 toms. in 8 vols., Vol. II [*De personis*] Romae: apud aedes Universitatis Gregorianae, 1928), II, 688.

[80] Lib. III *decretalium Gregorii IX,* tit. 50.

it by the commentators[81] it can be seen that the terms chancellor, notary, actuary and *tabellio* were all used to designate that public person who was appointed to do the notary work of the episcopal chancery from the thirteenth century on.[82]

Although this curial notary of the bishop's chancery is not exactly the diocesan chancellor who is found in the general law of the present day, yet the practice of having a public person in the diocesan curia with *ecclesiastical,* not *civil,* authority is now firmly established. That this public person was sometimes called *chancellor* began a custom which eventually became so established that the general law in 1918 finally determined that there should exist a legal office by this name in the diocesan curia for the exercise of the ecclesiastical power of notary. Though the chancellor had often cared for documents, the development of the organized diocesan archives did not take place until after the fifteenth century, as will be shown in the next chapter. Then it was that he became in practice also the custodian of the archives. This practice gradually developed into the general custom that finally led the general law for the first time in 1918 to set up the legal office of chancellor with a double function: that of public notary in the curia, and that of custodian of the diocesan archives.[83]

---

[81] Schmalzgrueber, *Ius ecclesiasticum universum* ([?] ed., 5 vols. in 12, Romae, 1843-1845), pars I, p. 13; De Lugo, *Disputationum de iustitia et de iure* libri duo (2. ed., 2 vols., Parisiis, 1670), disp. XLI, vol. II, pp. 620-623; Bouix, *Tractatus de judiciis ecclesiasticis* (2 vols., Parisiis, 1855), I, 482-496; Lega-Bartoccetti, *op. cit.,* I, 147.

[82] Cf. Couly, *"Les notaires ou actuaires,"—Le Canoniste,* XLVII (1925), 78; also Maupied, *Compendium iuris canonici* (2 vols., Parisiis, 1863), I, 826.

[83] Can. 372.

CHAPTER III

Historical Development From the Sixteenth Century

ARTICLE 1. THE SIXTEENTH CENTURY PARTICULAR LEGISLATION

In the sixteenth century there is to be found what seems to be the *first definite and clear legislation,* though it is only a particular law, which establishes the function of the diocesan chancellor to be what it is in the present-day Code of Canon Law. This is found in the III Provincial Council of Milan (1753),[1] which had great influence on the particular laws that were passed in other countries by bishops who followed the lead of St. Charles Borromeo. This legislation of Milan will be investigated shortly.

The Council of Trent gave the impetus to the particular legislation of this century. This council was held from the year 1545 to 1563, and in all its various sessions it makes no mention of a chancellor of the diocese, but it does renew the provision of Pope Innocent III, recalling to the bishops that they have the power to establish a notary in the curia.[2] This no doubt had an effect on the legislation of the Council of Milan and of other particular councils, for St. Charles Borromeo himself stated that he

[1] *"De iis quae ad Episcopale forum pertinent," III Conc. Prov. Mediolen. a. 1573*—Ratti [Pope Pius XI], *Acta Ecclesiae Mediolanensis* (3 vols., Milan, 1890-1892), II, 275. (Hereafter this collection will be cited as Ratti, *Acta.*)

[2] Sess. XXII, *de ref.,* C. 10.

called his first council at Milan to put into effect the decrees of the Council of Trent,[3] and the Council of Rheims, which was held about two years after the celebration of Session XXII of the Council of Trent enacted legislation on the notary by defining the duties of the notary in the better administration of authentic documents,[4] as did also a Council of Toledo in Spain which in 1655 made a law on the diocesan notary giving to him the care of documents.[5] But neither in these two particular councils, nor in the General Council of Trent, was there any definition or even a mention of the office of diocesan chancellor as such.

At Milan, however, there is found for the first time any direct legislation on the chancellor. It seems to be the model for the definition of the office in the Code of 1918.

In the I Provincial Council of Milan (1565) the documentary system is not differentiated from its earlier development in the previous centuries. Laws were made for notaries, scribes and chancellors without any distinction being indicated between the particular differences that attached to the curial work with documents as performed by these various officials.[6] In legislating on the inventories of ecclesiastical goods that were to be kept in the archives of the Cathedral, this council made no mention of the chancellor as archivist. One key of the archives was to be given to the bishop and the other to the chapter.[7]

---

[3] Ratti, *Acta,* II, 1.

[4] Council of Rheims (1564)—Mansi, XXXIII, 1365.

[5] Act. III, ad primum, Council of Toledo (1565)—Harduin, X, 1159.

[6] "Quaecumque de notariis sancita sunt, iis etiam scribas et cancellarios tenere volumus," *Pars secunda constitutionum, de notariis et scribis*—Ratti, *Acta,* II, 87.

[7] "Archivia singula duabus clavibus occludantur. In ecclesiis cathedralibus, earum unam Episcopus, alteram Capitulum servet"—Ratti, *Acta,* II, 113.

It seems that the dioceses had neglected to keep up the archives in the cathedral, for this same council ordered them to be erected in those suffragan sees where they did not exist.[8]

Four years later at the II Provincial Council of Milan (1569) it was still the duty of a member of the chapter to care for the archives, as is evident from the legislation on the custody of the archives on the occasion of the death of the bishop.[9] The law was copied almost exactly from the legislation of the Council of Toledo mentioned above.[10] Again in the II Council of Milan a decree was given which contained a list of the documents to be prepared by the notary[11] and enumerated practically the same ones that the decretalists speak of as being the work of the chancellor to prepare.[12] At the same time another decree pointed to the notary in the episcopal chancery as being distinct from the custodian of the archives.[13] Thus up to this council the chancellor's office was not defined any differently than in previous centuries.

But then came the change in the legislation already referred to. A clear concept of the diocesan chancellor, as in today's general law, was established in the particular legislation of the III Provincial Council of Milan (1573).

---

[8] "At vero in quibus ecclesiis vel cathedralibus, nec ne collegiatis archivium eiusmodi non sit, ab Episcopo instituatur"—*loc. cit.*

[9] "Cum primum aliquis hujus provinciae episcopus mortem obierit, Archivi Episcopalis claves, notarii publici fide, una Capituli vicario, altera uni de Capitulo, ad quem vel officii ratione, vel consuetudine pertinet," Tit. II, decr. XIV—Ratti, *Acta,* II, 197.

[10] Actio III, decr. I, of the Council of Toledo (1565)—Harduin, X, 1159.

[11] Tit. III, decr. XVII—Ratti, *Acta,* II, 197.

[12] Cf. Prosper Fagnanus, *Commentarium in decretalium libros,* lib. III, tit., 50, n. 8.

[13] Tit. III, decr. XII—Ratti, *Acta,* II, 197.

A decree of this council ordered the curial documents to be preserved in the episcopal archives under the care of the chancellor who was to keep the key to them.[14] The Council also defined the chancellor's position as notary. In this legislation for the first time he was defined as a notary for the bishop in administrative procedure, as someone distinct from the other curial notaries or actuaries who functioned in judicial procedure. The ordinary notaries of the curia take down the testimony in contentious trials and prepared the written instruments of the tribunal, while *only the chancellor* was to act as notary in those things in which the authority or a decree of the bishop was interposed.[15]

Here it is that is found the development of legislation which changed from an indefinite manner of speaking of the chancellor along with other notaries and scribes without ever mentioning their specific differences in the first Provincial Council, to a definite and specific reference to the chancellor as the custodian of the curial archives and administrative notary of the Bishop in the third Provincial Council in Milan. Thus for the first time in any legislation that can be found, the office of diocesan chancellor is firmly established in a particular law as it is now defined in the universal law of the

[14] "Certus in archivo Episcopali locus constituatur, ubi causarum ac judiciorum codices, instrumenta, acta scriptave alia cancellario et a notariis . . . recordantur. Is certus archivi locus duabus clavibus claudatur, quarum unam Episcopus, alteram ejus cancellarius habeat," *De iis quae ad Episcopalem forum pertinent, III Conc. Prov. Mediolen.*—Ratti, *Acta,* II, 275.

[15] "Testium dicta, et attestationes, in causis civilibus [contensiosis] ne scribantur ab alio quam ab ipso causae Notario sive Actuario, vel ab alio eius nomine; . . . idem decernitur de instrumentis, actisve dictae causae, quibus decretum judicis adscribi contigit. In aliis vero omnibus, quibus auctoritas, decretumve Episcopi sit interpositum, *Cancellarius tantum* notarius adhibeatur."—Ratti, *Acta,* II, 276.

Church. In later councils at Milan (1576 and 1579) it continues to be so defined and is permanently established.[16]

ARTICLE 2. PARTICULAR LEGISLATION TO THE END OF THE EIGHTEENTH CENTURY

Together with this legislation of Saint Charles Borromeo (1538-1584) there seems to have been a new interest in other legislation concerning the care of archives in various places. In the year 1571, Pope St. Pius V (1566-1572) gave directions to the bishops of Sicily about archives in order to correct abuses and laxity that had arisen.[17] Then in the year 1587, Pope Sixtus V (1585-1590 extended the legislation for the care of archives to the whole of Italy.[18] About this time there also is found legislation in Mexico in regard to the diocesan chancellor as an archivist-notary. This is in the III Council of Mexico (1585). It introduced to the Spanish Americas the office of diocesan chancellor according to the Councils of Milan.[19] However, from the sixteenth to the eighteenth centuries the term *chancellor* was not yet employed universally for the custodian of the diocesan archives.

---

[16] Cf. Ratti, *Acta,* II, 276 and 1700.

[17] Const. *"Muneris nostri,"* 1 mart. 1571—*Bullarium diplomatum et privelegiorum sanctorum romanum pontificum Taurinensis Editio* (24 vols. & app., ed. a Francisco Gaudé, Augustae Taurinorum, 1857-1872), VII, 893. Hereafter cited as *Bullarium Romanum Taurinense.*

[18] Instructio *"Provida,"* 29 apr. 1587—Quaranta, *Summa bullarii earumve summorum pontificum constitutionum* (Venetiis, 1622), p. 88.

[19] "Officium insuper creamus cancellarii . . . qui . . . annotet et scribat et instrumenta custodiat . . . ," stat. 17—Harduin, X, 1741; cf. also Du Cange, *Glossarium totius latinitatis,* II, 143.

Such names as *secretary,*[20] *custodian,*[21] or archivist were often used in the legislation to designate the person who had the diocesan archives under his care.[22]

The particular legislation, especially that which is reflected in the private replies of the Holy See from the seventeenth century onward is found to use the term *chancellor* more and more frequently in connection with the questions dealing with the care of diocesan documents. The chancellor is spoken of as the notary of the curia more often than the archivist.[23] Pallottini himself says that the chancellor is accepted as a public notary in the "resolutions" of the Congregation of the Council from 1625 to 1825 with regard to all the documents of the diocese, but that it is not known when, or if, this was ever stated in any general law, namely, that the diocesan chancellor was a legally accredited notary public. It was accepted through practice that he should be made one by the bishop.[24] The replies of the Congregation not only show that the diocesan chancellor was accepted as the notary of the bishop in practice, but they also imply that it was the

---

[20] Council of Rouen (1589), "de juridictione ecclesiastica," n. 9—Harduin, X, 1255.

[21] Council of Naples (1699), cap. II, n. 10—*Acta et decreta sacrorum conciliorum recentiorum, Collectio Lacensis* (7 vols., Friburgi Brisgoviae, 1870-1890), I, 238. (Hereafter this collection will be cited as *Coll. Lac.*)

[22] Benedictus XIII, const. *"Maxima Vigilantia,"* 14 iun. 1727, n. 23—*Bullarium Romanum Taurinense*, XXII, 566.

[23] This legislation can be found in Zamboni, *Collectio S. Congregationis concilii* (4 vols., Atrebati, 1860-1868), s.v. "Cancellarius," I, 313; also in Pallottini, *Collectio omnium conclusionum et resolutionum apud sacram congregationem cardinalium S. Concilii Tridentini* (18 vols., Romae, 1868-1896), "Notarius seu Cancellarius," IV, 361-372. (This work is hereafter cited as Pallottini, *Collectio.*)

[24] Pallottini, *Collectio,* XIV, 361.

chancellor who acted as the custodian of the archives in the diocesan curia. In settling a discussion as to whether certain documents were to be kept in the archives of the commune or in the bishop's archives, this Congregation stated that it was the practice and discipline of the Church for the documents drawn up by the bishop's chancellor to be kept in the episcopal archives under the care of the chancellor. The Congregation speaks of a decree of 1625 which supported this practice and then ordered the documents that had been prepared by the bishop's chancellor to be taken from the communal archives and to be returned to the diocesan chancery.[25] The ordinary judicial notary in the curia was never spoken of as a custodian of the archives, and it appears that this function belonged to the chancellor. For instance, a decree of the Sacred Congregation of Bishops and Regulars, in 1600, ordered the tribunal notary to send the documents of the trial to the chancellor for the bishop's archives.[26] But the chancellor on the other hand was often employed as a tribunal notary.[26a]

In the year 1727, Pope Benedict XIII (1724-1730) promulgated an important constitution on the care of the diocesan archives. In it he brought to the attention of the bishops of Italy the duty of the chancellor in regard to the custody of the documents in the archives.[27] It was

---

[25] Pallottini, *Collectio,* s.v. "Instrumenta," n. 26, X, 561-564.

[26] S. C. Ep. et Reg., decr. 16 oct. 1600, n. 11—*Codicis iuris canonici fontes cura Emi. Petri Card. Gasparri editi* (9 vols., Romae [later, Civitate Vaticana]: Typis Polyglottis Vaticanis, 1923-1939. Vols. VII-IX ed. cura et studia Emi. Justiniani Card. Serédi), n. 1586, § 11. (Hereafter this collection will be referred to as *Fontes.*)

[26a] Cf. Bouix, *Tractatus de judiciis ecclesiasticis,* I, 480; Roberti, *De processibus* (2 vols., Romae, 1926), I, 186.

[27] Benedictus XIII, const. *"Maxima Vigilantia,"* 14 iun. 1727—*Bullarium Romanum Taurinense,* XXII, 560-567; *Fontes,* n. 293.

this constitution that the Code of 1918 followed in regard to its provision concerning the diocesan chancellor as archivist.[28] In this constitution of Pope Benedict XIII, which was binding only in Italy, the office of the diocesan chancellor is treated as an office which involved the double function of an administrative notary and of an archivist.[29] The chancellor who cared for the archives of the bishop as the curial notary was distinguished from the ordinary notary who had to prepare the inventory of the seminary archives.[30]

Other particular legislation of the eighteenth century also shows that the bishop's chancellor had the double function of caring for the documents in the archives as well as of acting as the administrative notary of the bishop.

In a provincial synod of the Ruthenians in 1720 the chancellor's work was recognized as an office which involved his duty of being notary and also his duty of retaining and caring for the acts of trials, for the lists or ordinations, and for the records of visitations, rescripts and dispensations. A tax list was given in accordance with which the chancellor could require a fee for the making of copies of certain documents.[31] In 1736 the

---

[28] This is the legislative source to which reference is made in the annotations to canon 372 on the chancellor.

[29] *Ibid.*, nn. 5 et 10: "Episcopi . . . catalogum et inventarium a notario seu cancellario curiae episcopalis . . . confici curent." "Eadem archiva duabus clavibus, et seriis inter se diversis aperiantur, quarum . . . altera a cancellario seu notario curiae episcopalis [servabitur]," *Bullarium Romanum Taurinense*, XXII, 561; *Fontes*, n. 293.

[30] *Ibid.*, n. 5: "In seminariis autem episcopalibus archivum, ut supra erigatur, et inventarium . . . per publicum notarium ab Episcopo eligendum, qui non sit cancellarius curiae episcopalis."

[31] Provincial Synod of the Ruthenians (1720), tit. VII—*Coll. Lac.*, II, 52.

same description of the office of chancellor was incorporated in the legislation of the Maronites.[82]

In private replies from the Congregation of the Council during the eighteenth century the chancellor is designated as the bishop's notary in assisting at elections in religious houses.[83] Pope Benedict XIV (1740-1758) wrote that it was the custom for the chancellor of the bishop to act as notary for diocesan synods.[84] Again, in a dispute about what documents and written instruments belong under the care of the bishop's chancellor, and whether they should be kept in the communal archives, the chancellor was declared to be the proper curial notary of the bishop in several replies of the Congregation of the Council from 1754 to 1758.[85] In 1781 in a diocesan synod at Ferrara the chancellor was designated as the archivist for the curial documents.[86] and in 1783 he is indicated as having charge of the diocesan archives. This appears from a reply of the Congregation of the Council to the diocese of Viterbo about a question of what was to be done with the curial documents in dioceses that had been recently divided. The chancellor was to transmit them to the diocese to which the documents pertained.[87]

From this particular legislation it is evident that the practice of employing the chancellor as the custodian of

---

[82] Provincial Synod of the Maronites (1736), pars III, cap. V, n. 2—*Coll. Lac.*, II, 330.

[83] S.C.C., *Tiburtina*, 26 apr. 1727—*Fontes*, n. 3325; S.C.C., *Wormatien.*, 17 sept. 1746—Pallottini, *Collectio*, XIV, 364; cf. also Zamboni, *Collectio*, I, 314.

[84] Benedictus XIV (Prospero Lambertini), *De synodo dioecesana* (libri 13 in 2 tom., Lovanii, 1763), tom. I, lib. IV, cap. I, n. III.

[85] Cf. Zamboni, *Collectio*, I, 314, n. 14.

[86] *Synodus dioecesana Ferrariensis, MDCCLXXXI* (Ferrariae, 1781), p. 273, n. XVI.

[87] S.C.C., *Viterbien. seu Tuscan.*, 11 ian. 1783—Pallottini, *Collectio*, s.v. "*Archivum*," n. 66, I, 506.

the archives and as the public notary of the episcopal curia was fairly well established by the end of the eighteenth century.

ARTICLE 3. FUNCTIONS OF THE CHANCELLOR IN THE LEGISLATION OF THE NINETEENTH CENTURY

During the nineteenth century the terms *cancellarius, notarius* and *actuarius* were still employed indiscriminately in some localities to designate the tribunal notary. Roberti says that, though it is the principal function of the chancellor according to the present universal law to care for the archives, yet before the Code the two functions of the notary of the tribunal and of the diocesan archivist were often placed on a par and thus were associated with the office of the chancellor.[38] Roberti attributes this usage to the fact that the Holy See in replies to the bishops often spoke of the chancellor *or* notary who was to be constituted for extra-judicial *or* judicial acts.[39]

In the middle of the nineteenth century Bouix wrote that in his time the terms *cancellarius* and *actuarius* were employed synonymously and at times confusedly by the canonists.[40] He himself, however, distinguished the chancellor from the notary and the actuary. The chancellor was *de facto* always connected with a certain curia or chancery.[41] Other commentators state that the term "chancellor" was often used in designation of the actuary in tribunal procedure. This is brought out in their

[38] *De processibus* (Romae, 1926), I, 186.
[39] *Loc. cit.*
[40] *Tractatus de judiciis ecclesiasticis,* I, 480.
[41] Bouix, *ibid.,* p. 481.

discussion whether it is necessary for the judicial notary or chancellor to be a cleric, or whether he can serve in that capacity as a layman.[42] Their doctrine shows at least that the chancellor continues to function as a notary though he may be not always a priest.

In the conciliar legislation of the nineteenth century the chancellor was occasionally mentioned as caring for the documents of the archives, though some of the councils made rules for the proper keeping of the diocesan archives without mentioning that the chancellor is their custodian.[43] In Italy the chancellor was definitely mentioned in particular legislation as being the custodian of the archives similarly as in the previous century.[44]

In the conciliar and synodal legislation of the nineteenth century many evidences that the chancellor continued to act as the administrative notary of the bishop can be detected from the fact of his subscription of the written decrees of the bishop as in the convoking of a synod or council, as well as in regulations dealing with the notary duties of the Bishop's chancellor. For instance, a chancellor of the bishop attested the episcopal letters opening the Council of Prague (1860).[45] The legislation

---

[42] Cf. Lega, *De iudiciis ecclesiasticis,* lib. I, tit, II, cap. I, art. 10; Wernz-Vidal (*Ius Canonicum,* tom. II [*De personis*], 688) say that the interpretation of the old decretal laws which prohibited clerics from acting as notaries should no longer be taken strictly. Cf. also Maupied, *Compendium juris canonici,* I, 845; Baart, *Legal formulary* (2. ed., New York, 1898), pp. 53-54.

[43] Council of Paris (1849), tit. III, cap. VIII—*Coll. Lac.,* IV, 25; Council of Bordeaux (1850), tit. IV, cap. X—*Coll. Lac.,* IV, 586; Council of English, Dutch and Danish colonies in the East Indies (1867), *decretorum sectio II,* n. 10—*Coll. Lac.,* III, 1114.

[44] E. g., *Lucanae ecclesiae synodus dioecesana* (Lucae, 1887), p. 309.

[45] *Coll. Lac.,* V, 386. A canon of the cathedral chapter sometimes performed this function of subscribing the bishop's letter of convoking a council, as in the Council of Rheims (1857)—*Coll. Lac.,* IV, 195, or in the Council of Vienna (1855)—*Coll. Lac.,* V, 121.

of the Plenary Council of Latin American Bishops held in Rome in 1899 commissioned the diocesan chancellor for the work of drawing up and authenticating documents in the curia of the dioceses of Latin America.[46]

The General Council of the Vatican (1869-1870) did not define the office of chancellor. It spoke of the notary and referred to the laws enacted by the IV General Council of the Lateran (1215)[47] and by the Council of Trent (1545-1563),[48] which laws ordered the appointment of notaries in diocesan curiae. But these laws made no mention of the office of chancellor as such; they dealt only with judicial notaries.[49]

Until the promulgation of the present Code of Canon Law there was no general legislation which directly treated of the diocesan chancellor or defined his office as it is now defined in canon 372. The development of the present law took place through particular legislation and by means of practical usage. These agencies gradually attributed the name of *chancellor* to the one who was the notary of the episcopal curia, and specifically to that notary who had care of the safe-keeping of the documents drawn up by all the notaries of the diocese.

When Pope Pius X (1903-1914) enacted rules for the care of the archives of Rome shortly before the preparation of the new Code of Canon Law, though he did not determine expressly that the chancellor was the

---

[46] Cancellarii munus est actus curiae nedum judicialia verum etiam extrajudicialia fideliter conscribere: actis, decretis, sententiis eorumque authenticis exemplaribus subscribere"—*Acta et decreta concilii plenarii Americae Latinae in Urbe celebrati, A.D. MDCCCXCIX* (Romae, 1902), n. 933.

[47] C. 11, X, de probationibus, II, 19. This was can. 38 of the Council.

[48] Sess. XXII, de ref., c. 10.

[49] *Acta et decreta S. Concilii Vaticani,* appendix, pars VI—*Coll. Lac.,* VII, 800.

official custodian of the archives, he made implicit allowance for the fact that they could be under his care.[50]

Immediately after this legislation the new Code was being prepared for publication. The annotations to canon 372 single out the Constitution *Etsi Nos* of Pope Pius X and the Constitution *Maxima vigilantia* of Pope Benedict XIII as the sources whence the present law in canon 372 is derived. These sources treated specifically the question of the care of archives, but did not define the office of chancellor. Since the lawmaker recognized the established *practice* of placing the diocesan archives in the custody of that notary who was the episcopal chancellor, he caused an office to be defined in the universal law of the new Code which was to have for its incumbent the *chancellor* of the diocese. What was already an established practice thus became the basis for a new universal law.

ARTICLE 4. LEGISLATION ON THE CHANCELLOR IN THE BALTIMORE COUNCILS

The particular legislation of the Baltimore Councils in the United States does not establish the office of diocesan chancellor until the III Plenary Council (1884), where the double function of curial notary and custodian of the diocesan archives was to be had in every diocese as connected with the office of chancellor.

[50] He spoke in general of the administrators who superintended archives. In the Constitution *Etsi Nos,* of January 1, 1912, Piux X stated in n. 80: "Administratorum, quibus tabularii vel archivi cura commissa est, munus erit acta et documenta recensere, custodire, ordinate servare, eorumque exemplar, recepto mandato, conficere et suis quaeque officiis tradere."—*Fontes,* n. 697. In this manner, the Pope enacted legislation concerning the archives in general, and not merely concerning those of the curia under the care of the chancellor.

In the year 1852 the I Plenary Council exhorted the bishops to set up a chancery in their respective dioceses.[51] This exhortation was repeated in the II Plenary Council (1866), which suggested at the same time that a chancellor and a notary be appointed for the drawing up of documents and for the purpose of taking testimony.[52] Finally the III Plenary Council (1884) ordered that a chancellor should be appointed to care for the archives and to act as the curial notary. He was to be employed by the judge as actuary in judicial procedure[53] and was to act as notary for the bishop. His notarial duties were mentioned in connection with several examples of administrative action. When the bishop proceeded in his investigation of a criminal action he was to employ the chancellor as his notary.[54] As bishop's notary, the chancellor checked the reports of the temporal affairs of the parishes when these reports were forwarded to the chancery by the priests,[55] he notarized the answers of the candidates in the *concursus* for permanent appointments,[56] and the priests could send to him their demands by which they sought payment of salaries past due.[57]

There are no other direct examples in the legislation of this council regarding the duties of the chancellor as notary, but it is clear that he was employed as the notary

---

[51] *Decreta Concilii Plenarii totius Amer. Septent. Foederatae, a. 1852,* decr. 7—*Coll. Lac.*, III, 146.

[52] *Concilii Plenarii Baltimorensis II Acta et Decreta* (Baltimorae: Murphy, 1894), nn. 71 and 75.

[53] *Acta et Decreta Concilii Plenarii Baltimorensis Tertii, A.D. MDCCCLXXXIV* (Baltimorae: Murphy, 1886), nn. 303, 305 and 311. (This is hereafter cited as *III CPB.*)

[54] *III CPB.*, n. 311.

[55] *III CPB*, n. 272.

[56] *III CPB*, n. 48.

[57] *III CPB*, n. 281.

of the bishop's curia. That the chancellor had also an important duty in the care of curial archives is demonstrated in the legislation according to which the archives were ordered to be arranged and cared for by the chancellor with the utmost of diligence.[58] Therefore, as far as the legislation goes, it is clear that the chancellor's office partook of the double function attributable to the office of archivist-notary.

But despite the lack of all mention of any other potential exercise of power on the part of the chancellor, either in the legislation of the Councils of Baltimore or even in that of the provincial councils that were held in Cincinnati, New Orleans, St. Louis, and New York, it is of common knowledge that the diocesan chancellor was continually employed in the capacity of an habitual and general delegate of the bishop. It is difficult to find an explanation for the origin of this practice in view of the lack of any documentary evidence. Indirectly it can be shown how this practice developed in part through the legislation of the II Plenary Council regarding the vicar general of the bishop who was to act only as a delegate of the bishop and who was to have precedence in honor over the clergy of the diocese.[59]

The vicar general had no power in the curia without delegation, even though he had a position of honor over the other priests. This position the bishop could grant to a prominent priest as a reward for good work in the

---

[58] *III CPB,* nn. 271 and 272.

[59] Vicarius Generalis, ab Episcopo designatus, eandem cum eo moralem gerit personam, eandemque ecclesiasticam constituit curiam; atque cum sit Archipresbyter, omnes alios in Dioecese Presbyteros et dignitates praecellit; nihil tamen potest sine Episcopi delegata potestate"—*Concilii Plenarii Baltimoren. II Acta et Decreta,* n. 72.

diocese without changing him from his parish or burdening him with additional responsibility. But at the same time the bishop needed a priest to help in the work of the curia. As a consequence, he would often delegate the chancellor with powers in the same manner in which decree 72 of the II Plenary Council of Baltimore permitted the granting of delegation to the vicar general.

Often a vicar general was already appointed as a delegate in another part of the extensive diocese or, if he lived in the cathedral city, he was busy with the work of a large parish. The bishop would then simply employ the chancellor as his delegate without giving him the name of a vicar general. This was convenient for the chancellor was more often at hand in the chancery office. And even though he acted as the bishop's delegate he did not have the precedence of honor over other priests that the law gave to the vicar general. In this way the bishop could, if it proved convenient, have in the curia even a younger priest who was the chancellor by name, but who was *in fact* also a vicar general in the exercise of delegated powers, without the likelihood of offending older and more worthy priests who might have been somewhat displeased if the younger priest had actually been named as a vicar general. Since the office of vicar general always denoted a mark of distinction, in virtue of the law of the council, the bishop was enabled to grant this office to a priest who was indeed worthy, but who could not always be burdened with the work that was necessary in the curia. Thus the custom arose of giving to the bishop's chancellor the delegation that was originally planned for the vicar general by the council. However, though the chancellor was not given a precedence of honor by law, his office nevertheless developed into a position of honor as a result of being the *de facto* vicar general in the exercise of jurisdiction, a vicar general *"in spiritualibus."*

This part of the II Plenary Council of Baltimore is now abrogated by the Code, for the powers connected with the office of vicar general are now *ordinary* powers. No longer can the chancellor have *de facto* equal powers with the vicar general. The latter's powers are *ordinary;* the chancellor's jurisdictional powers which he may have are merely of a delegated character if they approach the scope of those jurisdictional powers enjoyed by the vicar general. If the bishop would wish the chancellor to act with the same legal power that the vicar general holds, he would now have to constitute him simultaneously as his vicar general according to the norms of the sacred canons relative to the provision of this office.[60]

[60] Cf. *infra,* chapter IV. For a complete treatment on this office of vicar general see Compagna, *Il Vicario Generale del Vescovo* (Washington: The Catholic University of America, 1931).

CANONICAL COMMENTARY

CHAPTER IV

THE APPOINTMENT OF THE CHANCELLOR

ARTICLE I. AN ECCLESIASTICAL OFFICE

The diocesan chancellor according to the Code of Canon Law is one of a group of those officials of the diocese who, taken together, comprise what is called "the diocesan curia." It is the function of this curia to help the bishop in the rule of his diocese.[1] The help given by the curia to the bishop, whether it be in disciplinary, administrative or judicial matters, is not to be understood in the sense that it could go so far as to supplant the exercise of rule by the bishop himself. It can not usurp any of his powers, nor can it act contrary to his disposal of matters, nor again may it exceed the limit of the powers entrusted to each member of the curia by law. Yet it is a participation, at least to some extent, in the rule of the diocese.[2] The manner of participation in this rule and the amount of help to be given by each member is explained by the Code. Thus canon 372 explains and determines the function of the diocesan chancellor as to his part in the participation in the rule of the diocese. He is a priest whose chief duty is to keep the acts of the curia in the archives, to arrange them in chronological order and to make an index of

[1] Can. 363, § 1.
[2] ". . . opem praestant in regimine totius dioecesis."

them. He is also by his very office according to the provision of the law, a notary.[3]

The function of diocesan chancellor is truly an ecclesiastical office[4] because it is established by the Code independently of the will of the bishop and continues in its nature of an ecclesiastical office to exist even though vacant. In other words, it matters not whether the bishop has or has not appointed a chancellor in his diocese, the office as such is made existent by the provision of the general law even as the offices of the vicar general or of the diocesan *officialis.*

An ecclesiastical office in the law can be understood in two ways: in a wide sense and in a strict sense. Widely understood it denotes any function legally exercised for a spiritual purpose. Strictly understood, an ecclesiastical office is one that is permanently (*stabiliter*) constituted by divine or ecclesiastical ordinance, conferred according to the norms of the sacred canons, and having in it at least some participation in the powers of orders or of jurisdiction.[5]

Coronata holds that the jurisdiction in an ecclesiastical office understood in the strict sense is ordinary,[6] and since

---

[3] § 1, "In qualibet curia constituatur ab Episcopo cancellarius qui sit sacerdos, cuius praecipuum munus sit acta Curiae in archivo custodire, ordine chronologico disponere et de eisdem indicis tabulam conficere"; § 3, "Cancellarius est eo ipso notarius."

[4] "Est verum officium ecclesiasticum . . . definitur officium cancellarium, officium a iure"—M. Conte a Coronata, *Institutiones Iuris Canonici,* Vol. I (2. ed., Turini, 1939), n. 426. (This work is hereafter cited as Coronata, *Institutiones.*)

[5] "Officium ecclesiasticum lato sensu est quodlibet munus quod in spiritualem finem legitime exercetur; stricto autem sensu est munus ordinatione sive divina sive ecclesiastica stabiliter constitutum, ad normam sacrorum cononum conferendum, aliquam saltem secumferens participationem ecclesiasticae potestatis sive ordinis sive iurisdictionis"—Can. 145, § 1.

[6] *Institutiones,* II (2. ed., 1939), n. 972.

he states that the office of chancellor is constituted as a truly ecclesiastical office,[7] it follows quite logically that he simultaneously must hold that the office of chancellor participates in at least some measure in the possession of the *ordinary* jurisdictional power.[8]

The fact that the function of the diocesan chancellor is an office in the strict sense appears evident because all the requirements, according to canon 145, are present in the office of diocesan chancellor as constituted by the law. The Code has clearly ordained its establishment in canon 372 and has defined its functions, thus providing for its permanence independently of the will of the bishop. The office as such never ceases or becomes extinguished; it can become merely vacant. From the very nature of the function attached to it by law, namely, from the legally accredited and entrusted administration, care and authentication of episcopal jurisdictional documents, it has *at least some participation* in the rule or jurisdiction of the diocese.[9]

In ecclesiastical law the term "jurisdiction" refers to the *fulness* of the power of ruling, whether it exists as a legislative, as an executive and administrative, or as a judicial and interpretative function.[10] It is employed in

---

[7] *Ibidem,* I, n. 426.

[8] It is to be noted that in the definition of a strict ecclesiastical office the law does not demand that the jurisdiction belonging to the office must be *ordinary.* This led some authors to say that a strict office can exist with only delegated jurisdiction, e.g., Vermeersch-Creusen, *Epitome Iuris Canonici,* vol. II (5. ed., Mechlinae: Dessain, 1934), n. 742; Sipos, "Ad officium sacrum an requiritur potestas ordinaria"—*Jus Pontificium,* XVI (1936), 67. Coronata, *Institutiones,* II, n. 972, does not share this opinion and adds that he does not know why Vermeersch-Creusen say that delegated jurisdiction is sufficient.

[9] ". . . opem praestant in regimine totius dioecesis"—Can. 363, § 1.

[10] Cf. Prümmer, *Manuale Iuris Canonici* (4. ed., Friburgi Brisgoviae: Herder, 1927), p. 119.

this extensive sense in the present Code of Canon Law,[11] as is evidenced by the law's use of the term *regimen* in speaking of jurisdiction.[12] Therefore the office of chancellor can be said *at least in some degree*[13] to participate in some part of this fulness of the power of jurisdiction, in so far as the care and especially the legal authentication of jurisdictional documents is a necessary part of the proper administration of the Ordinary's jurisdictional power. Coronata likewise appears to agree with this argumentation that the function of the chancellor is an office in the strict sense. He says that the chancellor's office is truly an ecclesiastical office which can not be said of the office of other notaries.[14] For since the function of a notary is an office only in the wide sense of canon 145, and inasmuch as Coronata employs the term "office" in speaking of the notary, he implies concomitantly that the chancellor's office is an office in the strict sense; for he distinguishes the chancellor from the notary by saying, "The chancellor's office is a *true office,* which can not be said of the *office* of other notaries. It has already been mentioned that Coronata holds that an ecclesiastical office in the strict sense carries with it ordinary jurisdiction as granted by the law.[15] Therefore he also implies that the chancellor has some participation

---

[11] Roberti, *De processibus,* I, n. 38.

[12] E.g., "Potestas iurisdictionis seu regiminis quae ex divina institutione est in Ecclesia"—Can. 196.

[13] Ojetti claims that even the very smallest participation in ecclesiastical power would suffice.—*Commentarium in codicem iuris canonici* (4 vols., Romae, 1927-1931), IV, 4.

[14] ". . . est verum officium ecclesiasticum quod non potest de aliis notariis affirmari; definitur officium cancellarium a iure; officium notarii potest restringi ab Episcopo qui ipsos eligit"—*Institutiones,* I, n. 426.

[15] *Institutiones,* II, n. 972.

in ordinary jurisdiction as granted by the law. This ordinary jurisdiction of the chancellor can only be that which he has received from the law for the legal administration and authentication of the jurisdictional documents that issue from the Ordinary.

For indications in the Code which corroborate the argument that the chancellor participates at least in some degree in the power of jurisdiction, one can point to the use of the term *regimen* in the law and also to the law's demand that the chancellor must be a priest.

The Code speaks of the power of jurisdiction as being the same as *regimen.*[16] It also states that the chancellor in his capacity of a member of the diocesan curia helps the bishop in the *regimen* of the diocese. But, certainly the use of this term with reference to the bishop's rule signifies jurisdiction, and as such the chancellor is indicated by the law itself as participating at least to some extent in the exercise of the power of jurisdiction in the diocese.[17]

Another such indication is found in the insistence of the law that the incumbent of the office of chancellor must be a priest.[18] Inasmuch as no layman can by law exercise ecclesiastical jurisdiction,[19] and inasmuch as it is forbidden by law that a layman be appointed as chancellor, one of the reasons for this prohibition must be sought in the fact that the law considers the office of diocesan chancellor as participating to some degree at least in the exercise of jurisdiction.

---

[16] "Potestas iurisdictionis seu regiminis . . ."—Can. 196.

[17] ". . . opem praestant in regimine totius dioecesis"—Can. 363, § 1.

[18] Can. 372.

[19] Can. 118.

Since the office of diocesan chancellor has been established by the Code as a permanent and true ecclesiastical office through which the incumbent aids the bishop in the rule of the diocese, the appointment to this office must be made in accordance with the general law which governs the conferring of ecclesiastical offices.

ARTICLE II. THE SUBJECT OF THE OFFICE

With regard to the necessary qualities specifically demanded of the one who is to be appointed as chancellor, there is not much expressly stated in the law other than that the chancellor must be a priest. But since he has the care of important documents and also has the position of a notary, he must enjoy a good reputation and be above every suspicion.[20] This qualification appears to be an essential requisite for a chancellor's valid appointment, because from the very nature of his position as a *testis qualificatus* for the authentication of documents, the affixing of his signature to a written act or instrument makes it acceptable for the furnishing of full proof in the ecclesiastical forum.[21] If he were untrustworthy, then any recognition of the possibility of a valid appointment would simultaneously nullify the very concept of what is essential for the constitution of truthful testimony. But such a recognition can not be given as long as one insists, as one necessarily must, that an untrustworthy person is completely unfit to be esteemed as a qualified witness and entirely unsuited for lending authenticity to a document. Moreover, the actual loss

---

[20] Can. 374, § 4.

[21] Cf. canons 1812, 1813 and 1791.

of good name through legal infamy renders a person incapable of obtaining an office,[22] and the loss of good repute through factual infamy involves an equal disqualification.[23]

Another quality that appears to be needed in the chancellor from the nature of that part of his office that has to do with the care of archives and the ordered arrangement of documents, is the characteristic of being neat and systematic. His ability to type efficiently will prove to be of great help because of the many letters and documents that he has occasion to draw up. Coronata demands that he also have a knowledge of canon law, in order that he may more expertly fulfill his work.[24] That the chancellor should be a priest who is known not to be indiscreet or imprudent in the matter of speaking about curial business is evident. He often works with curial documents that may deal with subject matter of a secret nature, and he could do much harm by the general divulgation of any knowledge he received by his curial position.

The question of whether the chancellor may be a layman has been settled by the Code. This is the first time that a general ecclesiastical law has instituted an ecclesiastical office for the care of the curial archives and for the authentication of curial documents. In establishing this new office the law demands that the incumbent must be a priest.[25] The old law, which considered the

---

[22] Can. 2294, § 1: "Qui infamia iuris laborat . . . est inhabilis ad obtinenda . . . officia et dignitates ecclesiasticas."

[23] Can. 2294, 2: "Qui laborat infamia facti repelli debet a recipiendis . . . officiis ecclesiasticis."

[24] *Institutiones,* I, n. 426.

[25] Can. 372, § 1.

chancellor rather in the character of a civil notary who acted also in ecclesiastical affairs, ordered that he should be a layman,[26] but with certain reservations.[27] However, in practice this decretal law had not been looked upon as binding long before the codification of 1918,[28] and bishops in the United States considered themselves free to appoint either a priest or a layman as chancellor.[29] This custom was justified, because the reason for the prohibition of the old law had disappeared. At the time of the Decretals the office of chancellor or notary constituted a business—a *negotiatio*—and therefore was unbecoming to the clerical state. When this condition had changed in the ecclesiastical forum, it gradually became the custom for bishops to appoint clerics for the notary work in their own curia.[30] This practice was taken over into the present law, and as far as the chancellor is concerned he must always be a priest. The ordinary notary, though he should generally be a priest, may still be a layman when the condition arises that no cleric can be had.[31]

That the appointee to the office of chancellor should be a diocesan priest is evident, though the canons do not

---

[26] C. 8, X, *ne clerici vel monachi saecularibus negotiis se immisceant*, III, 50.

[27] C. 11, *de haereticiis*, V, 2, in VI°. (These reservations which permitted solely a cleric to act as notary or chancellor in cases of accusations of heresy prove the existence of the general prohibition against clerics to act in the capacity of notary.)

[28] "Ego autem testari possum omnes hodiernum Galliae Episcoporum cancellarios esse clericos . . . et in plerisque mundi catholici regionibus."—Bouix, *De judiciis ecclesiasticis*, I, 492.

[29] Baart, *Legal Formulary* (New York, 1898), pp. 53, 54.

[30] Lega-Bartoccetti, *Commentarius in iudicia ecclesiastica*, I, 149; Wernz-Vidal, *Ius Canonicum*, Tom. II, n. 644; Bouix, *ibidem*, I, 482.

[31] Can. 373, § 3.

explicitly exclude a religious priest from the exercise of this office. However, a religious appears to be indirectly prohibited by canon 626,[32] for the exercise of this function in the diocesan curia seems not to be compatible with the religious state. This is evidenced from parallel prohibitions placed on religious in the exercise of other curial positions. For if a religious may not act as procurator or advocate outside his own religious tribunal,[33] or perform the function of notary in the process of the beatification of saints outside a case of necessity,[34] or act as vicar general unless the diocese be committed to the charge of his own religious community,[35] because these offices are not in keeping with the religious state, so also, *a pari,* he seems to be prevented from filling the office of the diocesan chancellor. According to Coronata,[36] this prohibition seems not to hold if the diocese is committed to the charge of a religious community. This is also the view held by Toso,[37] who claims that if the vicar general can be a religious when the diocese is in the care of a religious group, *a fortiori,* in the same circumstances the chancellor can be a religious. D'Angelo on the contrary thinks that only a diocesan priest should be appointed even in this exceptional case.[38] A diocesan priest who was at one time a professed religious is forbidden to hold any curial office as that of the chancellor

[32] "Religiosus nequit . . . ad dignitates, officia aut beneficia promoveri, quae cum statu religioso componi non possint."

[33] Can. 1657.

[34] Can. 2014.

[35] Can. 367.

[36] *Institutiones,* I, n. 426.

[37] *Ad Codicem Juris Canonici Commentaria Minora,* Tom. III (Città di Castella, 1921), 19.

[38] *La Curia Diocesana,* p. 29, footnote.

without a special mandate from the Holy See. The reason for this prohibition should be sought in the desire of the Holy See not to encourage religious to become secularized rather than in the idea that a secular priest who was once a religious is not thought to be endowed with the qualities needed in curial work.[39]

ARTICLE III. CONFERRING THE OFFICE

The appointment of the chancellor should be given in writing. Canon 364 requires that all members of the curia receive their appointments in writing. However, this rule is certainly not set up as a requisite for the validity of the appointment, for the law does not state its requirement in the nature of an essential demand. Yet, the simply oral appointment of a chancellor would not only imply an unlawful procedure, but also would involve potential difficulties and invite stubborn perplexities, for without a written appointment to his office it could become a trying task for the chancellor to certify his authority if it were called into question. Such a difficult situation could readily arise if upon the bishop's death someone who wished to enter the archives would refuse to acknowledge the chancellor's authority in barring his desired entrance.

The bishop does not have to consult anyone in the appointment of the diocesan chancellor. However, according to the norms of the canons which give him the cathedral chapter or the diocesan consultors as a council to advise and help him in the rule of his diocese,[40] it

---

[39] Cf. can. 642.

[40] Can. 391; can. 423.

appears to be more in accordance with the spirit of the law for him to seek advice from this group if he have some doubt about the choice of a priest or about the aptitude of the prospective appointee to the office of chancellor.

The obligation of the bishop actually to fill the office of chancellor seems to be a grave one.[41] That he has some obligation is apparent from the wording of canon 372,[42] and is implied in the provision of canon 155 which demands that an ecclesiastical office be not allowed to remain vacant beyond six months.[43] That this obligation is at the same time a grave one appears evident from the nature of this office which has for its principal function the care of curial archives. The Church has strongly insisted on the serious obligation of carefully preserving the official acts of the diocese in the archives.[44] Unless the diocese were quite small, it would hardly be possible for the bishop himself to care properly for the archives along with his other duties. Even if such a situation did exist the bishop still needs the chancellor in the capacity of the notary designated by law for authenticating the written episcopal acts and for countersigning his decrees. It may be argued that this obligation can be cared for by another notary, and that the archive work can be sufficiently accomplished by some such person as a secretary or prefect. But these persons by such an assignment do not necessarily become incumbents of

---

[41] Cf. d'Angelo, *La Curia diocesana*, p. 30.

[42] "In qualibet Curia constituatur ab Episcopo cancellarius."

[43] "Officiorum provisio . . . nunquam differatur ultra sex menses utiles ab habita notitia vacationis."

[44] Can. 375; Benedictus XIII, const. *"Maxima vigilantia,"* 14 iun. 1827, n. 5—*Fontes*, n. 293; *"Etsi nos,"* 1 ian. 1920, n. 80—Fontes, n. 697.

ecclesiastical offices. The office of chancellor has actually been set up by the general law, and the law has ordered the conferring of this office for the very purpose which these other persons would serve in their assignment. The appointment of some person to serve in the capacity of secretary for the bishop can not be said to fulfill the demands of the canonical provision regarding the office of chancellor of the diocese. This provision of the law must be accomplished by adherence to the norms of the canon.[45] The appointment simply of a secretary or a prefect of archives does not fulfill the demand of the canons. The obligation of appointing a chancellor in accordance with the provision of law would still remain.

The vicar general can not appoint a priest to the office of diocesan chancellor without a special mandate from the bishop,[46] nor can he remove or suspend the chancellor who has been appointed by the bishop. This is evident from the law which says that the chancellor or the notaries can be removed or suspended by the one who constituted them in office.[47] Therefore, since the vicar general did not appoint the chancellor, he also can not remove him from office. This rule, however, seems not to hold true in the case wherein the bishop has given a special mandate to his vicar general for constituting a priest in the office of chancellor. In such a case it can not be said that this same vicar general would act invalidly, even without a special mandate, were he to remove the priest now in office by virtue of the fact

---

[45] Can. 147.

[46] Can. 152.

[47] "Cancellarius aliique notarii . . . omnes possunt removeri aut suspendi ab eo qui illos constituit . . ."—Can. 373. § 4 and § 5.

that he himself has legally appointed him. There is no express restriction in the law of the power of the vicar general in this instance. One may argue that such a removal would not seem to be in accordance with the spirit of the law. For if the vicar general can not remove even a parochial assistant without a special mandate,[48] and the administrator or vicar capitular need the consent of the consultors or chapter to remove the chancellor and the notaries,[49] it does not appear to be equitable that the vicar general should ever be able to remove the chancellor without a special mandate. Nor would it appear consistent, one may again argue, that the vicar general should appoint a chancellor by virtue of a special mandate and then remove him by his ordinary power. However, these objections do not show that the vicar general would act invalidly in removing a chancellor without a special mandate when he himself has legally appointed him. Canon 368 gives the power to the vicar general to exercise jurisdiction in all that pertains to the bishop by ordinary rule excepting those things which the bishop reserves to himself or which by law need a special mandate from the bishop. Certainly the law does not demand a special mandate in this instance, and therefore, unless reserved to himself by the bishop, the removal of the chancellor in this case by the vicar general is certainly a valid act.

When the bishop dies the office of the chancellor does not become vacant. The priest occupying this position continues to act in that capacity unless his appointment was made *ad beneplacitum*.[50]

---

[48] Can. 477, § 1.
[49] Can. 373, § 5.
[50] Can. 183, § 2.

If the diocese is being ruled by the *vicar capitular*, or by the administrator who has the same powers in the United States,[51] and the office of chancellor is vacant, there seems to be no prohibition to prevent this administrator or *vicar capitular* from both validly and licitly filling it. The *vicar capitular* enjoys the same ordinary jurisdiction as the bishop in spiritual and temporal matters in all things not expressly forbidden to him by the law.[52] Nowhere in the general law is he expressly forbidden to fill an ecclesiastical office, as is the vicar general. He has the actual power then to appoint a chancellor. However, according to the norm of "*sede vacante nihil innovetur,*" and because in practice the position of the chancellor is often of special importance in some dioceses, it would be certainly more prudent in these localities to leave the appointment of a chancellor for the time when the new bishop takes charge. Naturally, in the meanwhile, some temporary provision should be made for the care of the written acts and curial documents.[53] The *vicar capitular* cannot of his own authority remove the incumbent chancellor or notaries from office. However, if the chapter or the consultors, as the case may be, consent to the removal of the chancellor, then the *vicar capitular* or the administrator may proceed to remove him from office.[54]

When the law permits that the chancellor be removed

---

[51] *AAS,* XI (1919), 75.

[52] Can. 435, § 1.

[53] Lega-Bartoccetti point out that the law simply says that the *bishop,* and not that the *ordinary,* should constitute a chancellor, and therefore the *vicar capitular* ought not to constitute a permanent chancellor, but should only appoint a priest to act for certain acts or causes, or for a certain time.—*Commentarius in iudicia ecclesiastica,* I, 148.

[54] Can. 373, § 5.

from his office by the one who appointed him thereto, it simply points to the superior whose competence in the matter thus becomes acknowledged by the law. The law does not thereby enable the bishop to deprive the chancellor of his office without reason. According to the norms contained in canon 192 there are certain conditions that must be present in order that the bishop may licitly deprive a priest of his office of diocesan chancellor even when it is not a case of penal removal from office. The presence of these conditions is as a general rule easily verified in practice whenever the bishop desires to make a change in this office. All that is necessary is that there exist some kind of cause that, in the prudent judgment of the bishop, is considered as being a just cause, even apart from the accompanying fact of any delict whatsoever on the part of the chancellor. Of course there must be due regard for natural equity in the particular circumstances, that is, an appointment to some other office must be made in order to care for the priest who has been removed from his office, and, what is more important, the removal must be made in such a manner that it does not appear like a penalty when there has been no delict. This removal is not effective until the moment when it has been authoritatively intimated to the priest. Recourse to the Holy See against the decree of removal is indeed granted, if such would ever happen to be the desire of the chancellor, but the decree must nevertheless be obeyed immediately upon its authoritative intimation to the chancellor.[55]

---

[55] ". . . de amovibili, privatio decerni potest ab Ordinario ex qualibet iusta causa, prudenti eius arbitrio, etiam citra delictum, naturali aequitate servata, sed certum procedendi modum sequi minime tenetur . . . privatio

ARTICLE IV. OATH, SALARY, ASSISTANT TO THE CHANCELLOR

After receiving his appointment to the office, the chancellor must take an oath before the bishop that he will faithfully perform his work without any show of personal discrimination or preference.[56] The law demands this oath in view of the very nature of a chancellor's duty in the preparation and care of important written acts and documents which must be preserved without mutilation or change, inasmuch as any such act of alteration would naturally yield to an unrighteous advantage for some persons, or to a sinister disadvantage for others. The taking of this oath provides a forceful guarantee for the proper handling and safeguarding of these important papers. That the law considers this to be very important can be seen from the fact that the bishop is authorized to impose severe penalties on the chancellor for any fraud or misuse in the handling of curial acts or documents.[57]

The office of the chancellor is not strictly a benefice if there is no provision for an endowment (*dos*) connected with the office.[58] It is left to the bishop to determine the manner in which the sustenance of the priest who fills the office is to be assured. Custom in the United States has generally provided for a stated salary without any right of participation in a definite percentage of the

tamen effectum non habet, nisi postquam fuerit a Superiore intimimata; et ab Ordinario decreto datur recursus ad Sedem Apostolicam sed in devolutivo tantum"—Can. 192, § 3.

[56] Can. 364, § 2, n. 1.

[57] Can. 2406; cf. *infra,* chap. V, art. IV.

[58] Cf. can. 1409.

chancery fees or taxes.[59] The expenses of the chancery office are generally met by the taxes which are permitted to be imposed in the execution of the various rescripts and acts of voluntary jurisdiction that issue from the Ordinary through the chancery. The amount of these taxes is to be determined in the provincial council or in a meeting of the bishops of the province.[60] Added to this is the income which may be derived from the small fees that are paid on the occasion of the granting of dispensations.[61]

Since the salary of the chancellor can be considered as being among the expenses of the chancery office, it can be taken from these fees and taxes. However, it may often happen that the income received by the chancery office through these fees and taxes is hardly enough to cover the ordinary cost of stationery and office expenses, let alone the salary for the chancellor's support. This difficulty is sometimes solved by giving the priest in this office another function from which he derives his income, as for instance the duty of caring for the spiritual needs of a convent or hospital, or of assisting in the work at the cathedral parish. This practical arrangement for the support of the priest who is the chancellor does not appear to involve the chancellor in the holding of incompatible offices as long as the fulfillment of his duties outside the chancery still leaves him free to fulfill also all the duties which attach to the office of chancellor.[62]

If there be a necessity for it, the law permits that an

---

[59] Cf. Baart, *Legal Formulary*, p. 54.

[60] Can. 1507.

[61] Can. 1056.

[62] Can. 156, § 2: "Sunt incompatibilia officia quae una simul ab eodem adimpleri nequeunt."

assistant be given to the chancellor, but it makes no express demand that this assistant be a priest.[63] This necessity will arise when the chancellor has more documents to draw up and to care for than he can expedite with his own conscientious application and reasonable diligence. It would not be present if the chancellor, in giving most of his time to other functions not connected with his office by law, could not for this reason fully care for the work of properly drawing up, signing, classifying and filing the official chancery documents, and in consequence would wish to place this responsibility in the hands of a vice-chancellor. The law assumes that the necessity arises in view of the burden of the great amount of work arising only from those functions it enumerates as attaching to the office itself. This necessity can easily arise in a large diocese wherein the chancellor is continually occupied with the drawing up of letters and documents, and the sending out of affidavits and copies drawn from the archives. The actual care of the preparation of files and of classification of indexes for the archives can then be assigned to a vice-chancellor in the capacity of assistant or registrar.

Though the position of the vice-chancellor has been called by various names in the past, such as *scrinius, chartularius, cartophylax,* etc.,[64] the present Code speaks of him in the capacity of a *tabularius*. But the particular signification of this term in the past law denoted a person who was responsible as archival administrator or as curator in a depository of public documents (*tabular-*

[63] "Poscente necessitate, adiutor ei dari potest, cui nomen sit vice-cancellarii seu vice-tabularii"—Can. 372, § 2.

[64] Cf. Thomassinus, Pars I, lib. II, cap. CIV.

ium).[65] Therefore if the present law refers to the vice-chancellor with the equivalent term of *vice-tabularius,* the canon seems to indicate that his duties are concerned with the actual care of the archives and the proper surveillance of the documentary depository under the direction and superintendence of the chancellor, rather than with such other functions of the chancellor's office as the drawing up of documents, the countersigning of them, and the proper authentication of public written instruments. By his very office the chancellor is constituted a public notary for the diocese;[66] but the vice-chancellor is simply a *vice-tabularius,* and does not have a capacity of acting as a public ecclesiastical notary by law.

---

[65] E.g.: "Tum tabularium tum archivium duplex erit, secretum aliud, aliud non secretum . . . Administratorum, quibus tabularii vel archivi cura commissa sit . . ."—Pius X, const. "*Etsi nos,*" 1 jan. 1912, nn. 78 and 80; "In secreto tabulario episcopali"—*Acta et Decreta Concilii Plenarii Americae Latinae in Urbe Celebrati, A.D. MDCCCXCIX,* n. 851; cf. also can. 375, § 1.

[66] Can. 372, 3.

CHAPTER V

Duties of the Chancellor as Deriving From the General Law

ARTICLE I. INTRODUCTION

Since the time of Pope Innocent III (1198-1216), when a *public person* in the capacity of notary was to be established in every diocese,[1] there have been one or more persons in the diocesan curia who alone by ecclesiastical authority had the power to authenticate documents by their signature. These public persons, whether they were called by the names of notary, actuary, chancellor, *tabellio* or *scrinarius* merited public credence (*fides publica*) by their very appointment for this work by the legitimate ecclesiastical authority. At the same time there were those persons in the curia who had the duty of caring for documents, especially since the early part of the eighteenth century, when archives were ordered to be set up in the dioceses of Italy.[2] Whether this function was also taken care of by those who acted as curial notaries or whether it was done by others who were especially appointed for this task under the names of archivist and *tabularius,* mattered little because the general law had not yet provided for these functions

---

[1] ". . . ut tam in ordinario iudicio quam extraordinario, iudex semper adhibeat aut publicam personam aut duos viros idoneos qui fideliter universa iudicii acta conscribant . . ."—C. 11, X, *de probationibus,* II, 19.

[2] Benedictus XIII, const. *"Maxima vigilantia,"* 14 iun. 1727—*Bullarium Romanum, Taurinense,* XXII, 566; *Fontes,* n. 293.

under one office. Sometimes an archivist was also appointed as curial notary; sometimes a chancellor or notary also cared for the documents; and sometimes different persons performed the separate functions distinctly, even in the same curia. There was, before the codification of 1918, no universal law combining both these functions and demanding that they be exercised in the curia under one distinct office.[8]

But with the advent of the Code there was established an ecclesiastical office which by general law had not existed before. The Code combined within one office the work of the curia which had been previously performed by persons variously termed as notaries and archivists. This office was called that of the diocesan chancellor. Through this office the chancellor was given by law the function of caring for the documents of the curia in the archives, and was recognized by the law to possess the status of a public ecclesiastical notary. If the diocese is to have any other notaries, they must be appointed specifically as such by the competent superior before they enjoy that capacity. But the chancellor is by his very appointment, not only the publicly recognized custodian of the archives, but also a public notary accredited with full ecclesiastical authorization to witness, to countersign, and thus to authenticate public ecclesiastical documents.

The chancellor is not simply an archivist, nor is he simply a notary. It is the combined functions of both of these in one and the same ecclesiastical office that pertain

---

[8] These few facts are evidenced from a perusal of some of the curial documents and particular laws of dioceses in past history. This matter is treated at greater length in the first part of this work.

to him in his capacity of chancellor. To give the name of diocesan chancellor to a priest who does not actually function in this double capacity would not harmonize with the intent of canon 372, which gives to the chancellor only the duties of superintending the curial archives and of acting as the public ecclesiastical notary of the curia. A priest who is appointed to this office and not meant for the carrying on of the functions of notary and archivist in the diocese, is also not meant for the performing of the work of the diocesan chancellor, even though he may have this office in name. By his very appointment to be the diocesan chancellor makes him to be the diocesan archivist-notary.

ARTICLE II. THE CHANCELLOR AS ARCHIVIST

Since the office of diocesan chancellor has been instituted to provide for the proper care of curial acts in the archives of the diocese,[4] the intention of this article is to explain: A, what by law are considered to be curial acts; and B, how they are to be cared for by the priest who is the diocesan chancellor. It is not the purpose of this article to discuss diocesan archives in general, their establishment, the care of them, or their arrangement. These topics have been fully expounded in a recent work.[5]

A. Canon 372 which details the duties of the diocesan chancellor, does not specify what constitutes the acts of

---

[4] ". . . cancellarius . . . cuius praecipuum munus sit acta Curiae in archivo custodire . . ."—Can. 372, § 1.

[5] Louis, *Diocesan Archives,* Catholic University of America Canon Law Studies, n. 137 (Washington, D. C.: The Catholic University of America Press, 1941).

the curia. But in other places the Code employs the term "acta" for various kinds of legal writings. For instance, the word "acta" stands practically identified with the word "instrumenta."[6] Instruments signify, in the canonical sense, written documents which are drawn up with a view to making possible the establishment of proof which may be needed in the future. These documents may be of a public or of a merely private nature according to their capacity or lack of capacity to furnish full judicial proof.[7] The term "acta" is applied also to *documents*[8] as well as to the authoritatively recorded minutes of any ecclesiastical procedure, whether such a procedure refer to a simple summary process,[9] or whether it refer to a formal ecclesiastical trial.[10] And finally, the law includes under this term all those official writings which have to do either with the spiritual or with the temporal business of the diocese,[11] such as any letters of ecclesiastical import, contracts, wills, etc.[12]

Not all the written acts of a diocese come under the direct care of the chancellor. Canon 372 speaks only of the acts of the curia. There may be other writings,

---

[6] Can. 374, § 1, n. 1 and n. 3.

[7] Lega-Bartoccetti, *Commentarius in iudicia ecclesiastica,* II, 781; Blat, Commentarium textus codicis iuris canonici, II (Romae, 1921), n. 411.

[8] Can. 1813.

[9] Can. 1990 and 1991.

[10] Canons 1585, 1587 and 1591 furnish some examples of this usage. All the written acts of a formal trial are called *"acta,"* but one may distinguish between the *acta causae* and the *acta processus,* that is, between the acts which relate to the merits of the question at issue, e.g., the written verdict and the recorded evidence in the case, and, on the other hand, the acts which relate to the procedural formalities in the case, e.g., the judicial citations, notifications, etc.—Cf. can. 1642, § 1.

[11] Can. 375, § 1.

[12] Can. 1813, § 3.

which are likewise to be conserved in the diocesan archives, but which are not of this group. What therefore does the law mean by the *curia* of the diocese?

As the word *curia* is ordinarily used today with reference to diocesan administration, it may signify two distinct concepts. It may mean only that group of persons, taken together, to whom is entrusted the duty of helping in the administration of the affairs of the diocese both in the judicial and the extra judicial procedures; it can mean also the place, office or building where these matters are generally expedited.[13] However, when the Code employs this term in relation to the diocese, it is used in the first signification of a group of persons,[14] who are explicitly named.[15] Therefore the official writings of these individuals are subject matter for the archives in care of the chancellor, depending upon whether they are considered worthy of being preserved according to the judgment of the bishop.[16]

Though, strictly considered, the bishop himself is not a member of the diocesan curia, his official writings may be considered as a part of the acts of the curia that are to be in the custody of the chancellor. By the very fact that they are *official* they pertain to the curia. If the writings

---

[13] Cf. Maroto, *Institutiones Iuris Canonici* (2 vols., Romae, 1919), II, p. 228, n. 824.

[14] "Curia dioecesana constat illis personis . . ."—Can. 363, § 1.

[15] "Quare ad eam pertinent Vicarius Generalis, officialis, cancellarius, promotor iustitiae, defensor vinculi, synodales iudices et examinatores, parochi consultores, auditores, notarii, cursores et apparitores."—Can. 363, § 2.

[16] Canon 375 says that those writings which are *needed* for the business of the temporal and spiritual administration of the diocese must be kept. It is for the bishop alone to determine what papers or documents are to be preserved. Cf. Louis, *Diocesan Archives*, p. 50.

of the persons who only help in the administration must be cared for, then *a fortiori* does this apply to the writings of the administrator himself. In fact the chancellor, the notary, or some other curial member often takes part in the drawing up of the bishop's documents, and by so doing directly occasions the classification of them among the curial acts. There are instances in the Code wherein it is specifically mentioned that certain documents of the bishop are to be kept in the archives. Among these, for example, are the official records pertaining to ordinations,[17] the attestations of the blessing or consecration of sacred places,[18] documents of the establishment of pious foundations,[19] and in general those documents of the bishop which relate to the spiritual and temporal rule of his diocese.[20]

In general, then, the writings under the care of the chancellor in the archives include all the written acts of the curia and the official written acts of the bishop, which may together be grouped under three headings: the writings that are received by the curia and the bishop, the copies of documents or of letters that are sent out, and the documents which are neither received nor sent out, but which circulate only in the curia, as for example the memoranda of verbal *proceedings* of which it is necessary to keep a record.[21]

It would be practically impossible to give in particular a list of every kind of writing which can fall under one

---

[17] Can. 1010, § 1.

[18] Can. 1158.

[19] Can. 1548.

[20] Can. 375.

[21] Louis (*op. cit.*, p. 50) gives this grouping from Jenkinson, *A manual of archive administration*, p. 23.

or the other of the above groups, and which the chancellor must care for in the archives. A few of the more notable writings that certainly pertain to the care of the chancellor can be named as follows: The acts of judicial procedure in the ecclesiastical forum; judicial sentences; precepts given to certain persons; decrees of the bishop; various letters, namely, of appointment, of financial business, of spiritual relations with the clergy and the laity, etc.; statutes; mandates for delegations; petitions for dispensations and favors; acts of the Synod; records of visitations, of the granting of benefices, of the erecting of parishes, etc.; a register of apostolic letters and the records of the execution of favors received from the Holy See; records which deal with religious, as for instance, the result of the *exploratio voluntatis novitiarum,* or permissions and dispensations granted to them; the material for the *ad limina* visit; signed professions of faith; records of the consecration of altars, churches and cemeteries; letters of approval for confessors; all the records of deeds of the various church properties, and the records of financial matters dealing with the whole diocese; these are but a few of the writings that must be cared for.[22]

When there is a question whether or not a certain writing is to be preserved by the chancellor in the archives, the bishop should be the one to decide, for with him rests the final responsibility of determining what should be preserved in the diocese. The Code gives him the norm to follow in such a decision by stating that those documents must be preserved which pertain to the

---

[22] Cf. Pignatelli, *Consultationes Canonicae* (11 vols. in 4 toms., Coloniae Allobrogum, 1700), consult. 210, n. 4, Tom. IV, p. 360; Louis, *op. cit.*, p. 23.

spiritual and temporal affairs of the diocese.[23] According to Louis[24] the principal purpose of archives is to assist the administrator in his work with a convenient form of "artificial memory," and an authentic evidence of the facts and events of his administration. They are not erected in the diocese for the information or the interest of posterity, and even though they may later be valuable to historians, this should not be a motivating reason for the bishop to keep certain writings. Instead, he should consider only whether or not the writing pertains to the business of the diocese, and whether, by being preserved in the archives, it will enable him to carry on the work of diocesan administration the more efficiently. By following this criterion, says Louis, the bishop will find it easier to avoid the two extremes either of cluttering up the archives with irrelevant material or of destroying papers or documents which are truly valuable and useful. Since this is the responsibility of the bishop, it is he alone and not the chancellor who is to decide about the destruction or preservation of any paper or document.

According to this criterion the bishop may give the chancellor permission to destroy the records of granted dispensations, for instance, when it is certain that a sufficient number of years have elapsed to make the need of keeping these records disappear altogether. Before destroying them the chancellor may simply record the pertinent names and the fact of the granted dispensation on a small card and file it away in a catalog of similarly preserved records. In this way useless writings that take up much needed space may be ridded, while at the same

---

[23] Can. 375, § 1.

[24] *Diocesan Archives*, p. 50.

time a record would still be kept that would be authentic by virtue of the authority of the chancellor who transcribed and signed the cards. The same thing could be done with much of the official correspondence of past bishops, when there is a certainty that the persons interested in, or the places treated by such writings can no longer exercise any equitable claims upon the preservation of such correspondence. Of course this may be done only after great care has been expended to ascertain all lack of any further equitable claims, and if it be thought wise to file away a small card-record of the essential characteristics of some of these writings, then great care must be taken in the accurate transcribing of the facts. This should be done by the chancellor, or by a notary, in order that the record can later be accepted as authentic. If the record be transcribed by a secretary, then it should at least be countersigned by the chancellor or a notary, in order that it may have the authentic value which ecclesiastical law connects with the documents or records which are properly signed by the one or the other of these persons in their official status.[25]

B. The exact manner in which the chancellor should care for the acts of the curia in the archives is not explicitly determined, other than that he shall arrange them in chronological order and make an index of them.[26] Thus the law wisely leaves the chancellor the opportunity to choose a system that may be peculiarly suited to the individual curia. Because dioceses differ so much in regard to the amount and kind of business that is transacted in the curia, it would be almost impossible for the

[25] Can. 373, § 1.
[26] Can. 372, § 1.

general law to set up a standard detailed system of caring for these archives which everywhere would be satisfactory. Since canon 372 has attached to the office of chancellor the duty of caring for these curial acts without definitely explaining how it should be done, it seems to be left to the chancellor's own ingenuity how this duty is to be best accomplished in his own particular curia under the prudent direction of the bishop. The final responsibility of the arrangement and care of the general archives rests with the bishop, and it is left to his ultimate judgment how this responsibility can best be satisfied as long as the writings are kept in good arrangement and are carefully enclosed.[27] Coronata suggests that the arrangement be determined by the bishop through legislation.[28]

Even though a chronological order of arrangement is asked for by canon 372, this does not mean that other systems, as for instance an arrangement according to subject matter, are excluded.[29] Evidently the bishop and the chancellor understand better than others what particular disposition of the arrangement and of the care of the curial acts will prove most practical in view of the local circumstances. Any convenient system that accomplishes the purpose of the laws on archives can be used. The present study does not propose to go into the details of any specific system for the care of archives, as this has already been done.[30]

---

[27] Can. 375.

[28] *Institutiones,* I, n. 428.

[29] Prummer, *Manuale Iuris Canonici* (3. ed., Friburgi Brisgoviae: Herder, 1922), p. 180; Augustine, *A Commentary on Canon Law* (8 vols., vol. II, 5. ed., St. Louis: Herder, 1928), II, 47.

[30] Cf. Louis (*Diocesan Archives,* pp. 52-55), gives a detailed description of a practical arrangement and index.

An important part of the care of the archives is that of their safe custody. The law is explicit in demanding that they should be kept locked with a key that should be in the possession of the chancellor. It also forbids ingress to them without the permission of the bishop or of the vicar general *and* the chancellor.[31] It would therefore be certainly illicit for the chancellor alone without the permission of the Ordinary to allow anyone to enter into the archives.[32] And although a person had permission from the Ordinary to enter, he must also receive approbation from the chancellor before he actually goes into the archives. Evidently the chancellor would not under ordinary circumstances refuse a permission granted by the bishop or the vicar general. However, because the chancellor himself by the very nature of his office has a grave obligation to care for the archives,[33] and inasmuch as his additional permission appears equally as necessary as that of the bishop or vicar general,[34] it is conceivable that in certain cases the chancellor can rightfully negate the previously granted permission of the Ordinary. The chancellor may, under circumstances unknown to the bishop, have intimate knowledge about the inadvisability of permitting a certain person from entering the archives. He could therefore not permit entry without violating his conscious sense of duty. He would withhold his permission until such time when he can approach the bishop for a

---

[31] "Archivum clausum sit oportet et nemini illud ingredi liceat sine Episcopi aut Vicarii Generalis et cancellarii licentia. Unus cancellarius illius clavem habeat."—Can. 377.

[32] Cf. Coronata, *Institutiones,* I, n. 428.

[33] Can. 372, § 1.

[34] Can. 377, § 1.

consideration of the matter. In all likelihood the bishop will revoke his previously extended permission. If he does not and the chancellor is still reasonably persuaded that his own permission must be denied, then his withholding of permission will suffice to bar the person's entry. The chancellor's acquiescence is of equal necessity with that of the Ordinary to constitute the requisite dual authorization for entry. The authorized withdrawal of even a single document from the place of the archives, presupposes the permission of the Ordinary,[35] and there must be left with the chancellor a receipt signed by the one who takes the document away.[36]

The importance of not detracting from the authority of the chancellor with regard to his grant of permission for entering the archives appears clear when one considers that on the death of the bishop it is the chancellor alone who has the responsibility of safeguarding the documents in the archives until the new superior is appointed. If it were customary to disregard, or at least to make little of, the demand that the chancellor *as well as* the Ordinary should give the permission for access to the archives during the reign of the bishop, then the danger would arise that the authority of the chancellor would not be sufficiently recognized by anyone who would desire very much to get into the archives after the death of the bishop. The chancellor has to be particularly vigilant during the time of the vacancy of the diocese, because he must see to it that no one, not even the diocesan administrator, will remove, destroy, conceal or alter any of the

---

[35] Can. 378, § 1.
[36] Can. 378, § 2.

documents of the archives.[37] The gravity of the chancellor's obligation at this time can be seen from the penalty that is imposed by the law in the way of an *ipso facto* incurred excommunication which for its absolution is reserved *simpliciter* to the Holy See, and from the further discretionary punishment of removal from office or benefice which the Ordinary may employ, relative to all who in their own person or through another have removed, destroyed, concealed or altered any of the curial documents.[38] The law also calls for the *ferendae sententiae* deprivation of office and for other proportionate and grave penalties to be imposed by the Ordinary upon all who are officially obliged to draw up, compose or preserve juridical acts, documents or record books either of the curia or of the parish, if they presume to falsify, mutilate, destroy or conceal them.[39] It is evident that any such malicious offense on the part of the chancellor would make him liable to the recounted penalties.

Any practice, therefore, that would minimize the responsibility attaching to the chancellor while the bishop rules in the diocese would only serve to jeopardize the proper care of the archives when the see is vacant, precisely because those who might wish to enter the archives would be inclined to consider the chancellor's refusal during the vacancy of the see to be no more decisive than they had learned to regard it before the bishop's death.

Though it is necessary to have permission from the chancellor in order to enter into the archives, the latter has no authority to grant permission for the withdrawal

[37] Can. 435, § 3.
[38] Can. 2406, § 1.
[39] Can. 2406, § 1.

of any document, or to refuse such a withdrawal when permission has been granted by the bishop.[40] The law does not even make any provision for the chancellor himself to take a document out of the archives on his own authority, but explicitly demands the permission of the vicar general or of the bishop every time this is to be done, and insists upon a signed receipt being left for the document when it has been permissibly withdrawn.[41] The care of the archives by the chancellor does not mean that he can deal with the pertinent documents outside the place of the archives, and were he to withdraw any of them even for a time he would be acting unlawfully.[42] Thus during the vacancy of a see it seems that *no one* may withdraw a document for use, even for a short time, outside the place of the archives. Since the chancellor cannot give this permission, and since the vicar capitular or administrator is explicitly forbidden to do so,[43] there exists no possible legal right for the withdrawal of any document from the archives for any reason whatsoever until the new bishop takes possession of the diocese. This prohibition can not be said to be placed also on the withdrawal of documents from the chancery, if these documents are not as yet filed in the place of the archives itself. Although the law makes no direct provision for the withdrawing or hiding of documents when the see is vacant, it cannot be concluded that even in an emergency this could not be done. Certainly there would be good reason for hiding the documents, for instance, were the chancellor to find out that a hostile civil authority

[40] Can. 378, § 1.
[41] Can. 378, § 2.
[42] Blat, *Commentarium*, II, n. 414.
[43] Can. 435, § 3.

plans to enter unjustly into the diocesan archives to examine and take away documents with a mind to do some harm to the Church. Though the Code does not legislate for such an extraordinary contingency and consequently makes no explicit provision for this circumstance, this would certainly be a sufficient reason for the chancellor himself during the vacancy of the see to remove the documents to a place of hiding. In case of grave necessity the law permits entrance into the secret archives (under certain safeguards) by another than the bishop,[44] and it seems that, *a fortiori,* the law indirectly permits the ordinary curial archives to be entered under the same conditions, for these do not have to be so secretly guarded.

That part of the archives which is termed "secret" is not placed immediately under the care of the chancellor by the law, but is most directly put under the care of the bishop himself.[45] The only duty that the Code gives the chancellor in regard to the care of the secret archives is that he should have custody of the key that belongs to the vicar general when that office is vacant or when he is not present.[46] The chancellor himself is never permitted access to this secret part of the archives. The law allows only the bishop or the apostolic administrator, no one else being present, to open or inspect them.[47] And

[44] Can. 382.

[45] Can. 379, § 1.

[46] Can. 379, § 3. The other key of the two that are necessary for opening the double lock of the secret archives is in the possession of the bishop. Blat (*op. cit.,* n. 415) says that the words *"eo deficiente"* in this canon can mean that the vicar general is simply absent, and not necessarily that his office is vacant.

[47] "Episcopus vel Administrator Apostolicus, repetita altera clave, ipse solus, nemine adstante, archivum vel armarium secretum, ubi opus fuerit, aperire et inspicere potest, quod deinde utraque clavi iterum claudatur."—Can. 379, § 4.

when the see is vacant, even the duty of safeguarding one key no longer attaches to the chancellor, for he must give up the key of the vicar general, if he had it, to the senior of the diocesan consultors or to the ranking dignitary of the chapter; and the former bishop's key is given to the administrator or the vicar capitular.[48] Before giving up these keys, the chancellor or vicar general and the priest who had the bishop's key[49] must seal up the secret archives,[50] and no one can enter them during the vacancy of the see except in case of grave urgency. Even in this case it is not the chancellor, but only the administrator or vicar capitular who may open them, and then only in the presence of two consultors as witnesses, who must see to it that nothing is taken away.[51] The chancellor therefore has very little part in the care of the secret archives as far as the general law is concerned.

ARTICLE III. THE CHANCELLOR AS NOTARY

By his very office the chancellor is a notary,[52] and therefore a public person whose writings and signature on a document are worthy of official trust.[53] His signature by the very authority of his office merits the same public credence before the ecclesiastical forum as does the testimony of two witnesses, according to the decretal of Pope Innocent III (1198-1216).[54] That the testimony under

[48] Can. 381, § 1, n. 2.
[49] Can. 380.
[50] Can. 381, § 2.
[51] Can. 382, § 1.
[52] Can. 372, § 3.
[53] ". . . Quorum scriptura aut subscripto publicam fidem facit."—Can. 373.
[54] ". . . iudex semper adhibeat aut publicam, si potest habere, personam aut duos viros idoneos qui fideliter . . . excribant."—C. 11, X, *de probationibus*, II, 19.

oath given by two or three witnesses who are above suspicion must be acceptable as proof, is an ancient procedure founded in the Old Testament laws[55] and firmly established in the present Code of Canon Law.[56]

Though the first signification of the term *notary* relates to the writing and taking of notes (thus *notary*),[57] it often means principally an official witness acceptable in law in view of his legal appointment to attest the authenticity of a document he subscribes. He may do the actual writing, or he may only add his signature to it after it has been written by another.[58] This notary is termed legally a *testis qualificatus*. His acts are accepted as authentic and are acceptable for the furnishing of full proof in the ecclesiastical forum.[59]

The authority of the notary to act in drawing up a document is limited to the territory of the superior who appointed him and can be exercised only for the enterprise for which he was rightfully constituted.[60] Therefore a notary appointed by one bishop could not act in the territory of another without a second appointment by this other bishop, although the acts drawn up by him in his

---

[55] "One witness shall not rise up against any man, whatsoever the sin or wickedness be. But in the mouth of two or three witnesses every word shall stand."—*Deut.* XIX, 15.

[56] "Si sub iuramenti fide duae vel tres personae, omni exceptione maiores, sibi firmiter cohaerentes de aliqua re vel facto in iudicio testificentur de scientia propria, sufficiens probatio habetur."—Can. 1791.

[57] Lega, *De judiciis ecclesiasticis* (2 vols., Romae, 1896-1898), I, 185, footnote; Bouix, *Tractatus de judiciis,* I, 482.

[58] ". . . quorum scriptura *aut* subscriptio publicam fidem facit."—Can. 373.

[59] "Unus testis depositio plenam fidem non facit, nisi sit testis qualificatus . . ."—Can. 1791, § 1; "In quolibet iudicii genere admittitur probatio per documenta publica . . ."—Can. 1812; ". . . documenta publica ecclesiasticia haec sunt . . . instrumenta a notariis ecclesiasticis confecta."—Can. 1813.

[60] Can. 374, § 2.

own territory are acceptable the world over in the ecclesiastical forum.

Therefore the signature of the chancellor on a document has the same legal effect in making it acceptable as authentic, as if he were appointed a notary for the diocese. The distinction between the ordinary notary and the chancellor with regard to their powers as a *testis qualificatus* consists only in the manner by which they variously receive these powers. Legal qualification of a witness can come only through the legitimate public authority. The notary receives his by appointment directly; the chancellor receives his from the general law by virtue of his office.

In the diocesan arrangement the chancellor as notary and the ordinary curial notary, though they have the same powers in the authentication of documents, do not function for the same persons nor do they act in the same matters. The chancellor acts regularly in the administrative procedure of the diocese, while the notary functions in the procedure of the tribunal. The chancellor draws up and countersigns the acts of the bishop, while the notary attends to those of the *officialis* or some other judge. Thus in many suggested forms for the drawing up of decrees, documents and other written acts, whenever it is a form for a written act or administrative decree of the bishop, a space is left for the signature of the *cancellarius*. When it is a form for the judicial decree or sentence of the judge, a space is left for the signature of the *notarius*.[61]

---

[61] E.g., Cappello, in his *Praxis Processualis* (Romae: Marietti, 1940), on pages 14-17 reproduces forms which serve for decrees of the bishop, and on which there is left a space for the *chancellor's* signature; and on pages 18-20 forms are listed for the use of the judge, and on which space is left for the signature of the *notary*.

This does not mean that the chancellor should not act in judicial procedure. Since he has the power of a notary, the judge may also select him for the notarial work connected with a judicial trial. But the chancellor must be especially appointed as notary for this or that special cause by the judge, and in being thus chosen the chancellor is constituted as an *actuarius* for that specific cause.[62] But neither the chancellor nor any other diocesan notary is by his appointment to office necessarily designated also as an actuary for any particular notarial function; both the one or the other become an actuary only by their selection by the judge, or through the previous designation of the diocesan Ordinary, for a specifically indicated case.[63]

It is not within the scope of this work to treat in particular of the ordinary tribunal notary as such. His duties consist in putting into writing and in authenticating all that is transacted in judicial procedure; besides he must draw up many documents, acts and instruments, and make copies or exemplars of them to be transmitted to courts outside the diocese.[64] But since the chancellor is also a notary, there are some things which are not ordinarily the work of the simple notary, and which remain for the chancellor to do in view of his official position. A few examples will be here given of notary work that pertains to the chancellor in as far as he is the custodian of the archives, and also in as far as

---

[62] "Cuilibet processui interesse oportet notarium, qui actuarii officio fungatur; . . . judex, antequam causam cognoscere incipiat, in actuarium assumere debet unum e notariis legitime constitutis"—can. 1585; cf. Bouix, *Tractatus de judiciis ecclesiasticis,* I, 480.

[63] Cf. Bouix, *loc. cit.*

[64] Can. 374.

he is associated with the Ordinary in some of the administrative procedure in the diocese.

One of the principal reasons for joining the function of notary to that of the archivist in the office of the chancellor seems to be that the one who cares for the archives should also be able to make authentic copies of them without the necessity of calling in a notary. Once a document is placed in the archives, it should be within the safe-keeping of the chancellor without the unnecessary danger of allowing it to be handled by others who might make alterations or lose it. Precisely for this reason is the chancellor simultaneously a notary, namely, that he himself can make any authentic copies needed from the archives without calling in another for this work. It is he, then, who should make authentic copies when they are legitimately petitioned, and not the ordinary notary. The chancellor's copies are acceptable for full proof in any ecclesiastical forum. In this way the originals do not have to be given to a notary, but always remain under the custody of the one who by the general law has the obligation to secure their safe-keeping, namely, the chancellor. Again, it may be necessary, for instance, to make notes on the margins of documents, or to write certain annotations in the indexes or files of the archives, concerning the acquisition or withdrawal of certain documents. These notations should be made and signed by the chancellor. They must then be accepted as authentic in consequence of his legal notary power. In this way the chancellor exercises his notary power directly for achieving the main function of his office, which is the care of the curial archives. No other notary needs to be employed for the transcription and authentication of the documents already contained in the archives. To do this work is one reason that the chancellor is given full competence as a public notary by the law.

The office of the chancellor can also be employed for expediting the functions of the administrative notary of the bishop. Because of the pressure of affairs it may be often more convenient for the Ordinary to issue oral statements of the granting of certain dispensations or in making certain decisions. Even without this reason there may also be a situation wherein it is necessary for the bishop to grant a dispensation when he himself can not sign it because of illness or because it is granted over the telephone. When the chancellor records this oral grant, signs it, and in sending it to the petitioner states the fact of the granting of the dispensation, or of the issuance of the decision, then this record of the chancellor is a public document[65] and furnishes full legal proof of the fact of the granting of that dispensation or of the issuance of the Ordinary's decision.[66] Once there is present the signature of the chancellor, then the legal presumption is in favor of the document as being genuine. Its credibility can be destroyed only by evident arguments that clearly prove the contrary. When the petitioner has received a notice from the chancellor the law does not permit him to doubt that it is genuine. Legally the petitioner will proceed just as if the bishop had personally written the grant of dispensation or decision and sent it to him. If he wishes to impugn the letter of the chancellor, he must have certain proof that it is not genuine despite its public character.[67]

---

[65] Can. 1813, § 1, n. 2.
[66] Can. 1816.
[67] Cf. canons 1814, 1816.

Even when the bishop himself signs important decrees or documents it is the function of the chancellor to countersign them, in order that there may be no question of their authenticity. The very office of notary which the chancellor exercises has been set up by the law to give public credence to documents. It constitutes a limit beyond which one can not any longer raise a further *legal* doubt concerning the essential facts contained in the writings as signed by this official. If this limit were not set by the law, then one might continually go on bringing up difficulties to throw doubt on the authenticity of all documents. Thus only definitely assuring proofs to the contrary, and not merely the obtrusion of some legal difficulties, misgivings or surmises, can discredit any writing that is signed by the chancellor. The possibility of a *legal* as distinct from a factual doubt cannot be extended to this notarized writing. Without such a provision it would be quite difficult ever to get certain proof from documents. One might always bring up the objection, "How can you be legally certain that what this document states is true, if you have no witnesses?" It is thus evident how important it is for a chancellor to be of great integrity and above every suspicion. The law accepts a letter with his signature as full proof of the facts for which it testifies.[68]

---

[68] "Cancellarius est eo ipso notarius"—Can. 372, § 3; "Documenta publica ecclesiastica sunt . . . instrumenta a notariis ecclesiasticis confecta"—Can. 1813; ". . . probatio admittitur per documenta publica . . ."—Can. 1812; "Documenta publica fidem faciunt de iis quae directe et principaliter in eisdem affirmantur"—Can. 1816; "Documenta publica . . . genuina presumuntur donec contrarium evidentibus argumentis evincatur"—Can. 1814; "Cancellarius aliique notarii debent esse integrae famae et omni suspicione maiores"—Can. 373, § 4.

There are here subjoined some examples for the notarial work of which, the bishop will ordinarily employ the chancellor, who in a particular manner is constituted as the administrative notary of the bishop.

The chancellor should countersign the appointment to ecclesiastical offices, which must be executed by the bishop in writing,[69] and the legitimate instruments of the erection of benefices[70] as well as the authentic writings which effect the union or division of benefices, bring about the translation of their see from one locality to another, or execute a territorial reallocation among benefices.[71] The decrees to be issued by the bishop should be drawn up by the chancellor and signed by him also, as a legal witness to the bishop's signature. This rule obtains, for instance, in the drawing up of decrees concerning the rejection or admission of a *libellus,*[72] concerning the nomination of a delegated judge,[73] or concerning the needed permission of the Ordinary to institute an ecclesiastical suit in certain instances.[74] In fact, any decree that issues from the bishop, and not from the *officialis,* should bear the counter-signature of the diocesan chancellor.

The special extra-judicial procedure which the bishop is called upon to employ in certain cases of the removal of pastors, or in the application of certain penal sanctions as provided for at the end of the fourth book of the

---

[69] Can. 159.
[70] Can. 1418.
[71] Can. 1428: *unio, divisio, translatio, dismembratio beneficiorum.*
[72] Cf. Cappello, *Praxis processualis,* p. 14.
[73] *Op. cit.,* p. 17.
[74] Can. 1526; *op. cit.,* p. 16.

Code.[75] demands the use of a notary who writes the acts of the whole procedure, which acts are then to be kept in the curial archives.[76] This is ordinarily the function of the chancellor. He must countersign the decrees for the designation of the examiners, for the renunciation of his parish by the pastor, for the calling in of witnesses, for the removal of the pastor, etc. He must also in drawing up the acts mention that the pastor was invited to leave his parish, put the testimony of the witnesses in writing, and also the discussion about the allegations produced by the pastor and the discussion about the recourse, etc.[77]

The chancellor is employed as a notary generally for those writings which proceed directly from the bishop. He is rarely appointed as tribunal notary. Therefore is he often spoken of as the notary of the bishop, and it is the chancellor who generally draws up those documents or those copies which the bishop must send to the Holy See.

In passing, one may well mention that on many occasions there is need of a civil notary public in the diocesan curia. Though this is of no benefit in strictly ecclesiastical procedure, yet for those things in which there is some connection with the civil law, as for example in the drawing up of deeds and contracts, it will be practical for the chancellor to be also a civil notary. This will save many visits for the bishop to a notary public and will obviate the need of bringing a civil notary public into

[75] Canons 2147-2194.

[76] Can. 2142.

[77] Cf. Cappello, *op. cit.*, pp. 141-174, for these forms as well as forms for the written acts to be used in the administrative procedure of applying the penal sanctions against clerics.

the chancery. There are also occasions on which a transcript of some document in the diocesan archives may be needed or asked for by a civil judge and then a notary public will be needed to make the transcript authentic for the civil law. The inconvenience of having to admit a notary public into the archives or also the temporary lending of an important original document can be avoided if the chancellor is also a civil notary public. This certainly is in harmony with the Code of Canon Law. For by canon 1529 the civil law prescriptions (that are not contrary to divine or ecclesiastical law) as affecting contracts are also to be observed by the Church. Thus if certain deeds in regard to Church property have to be notarized civilly according to the civil law, then a civil notary is also *demanded by Canon Law.* Canon 139, § 2, in forbidding clerics to function as notaries public *except in ecclesiastical curiae,* cannot be interpreted as forbidding the chancellor to be a civil notary public. It is the habitual functioning in the capacity of a civil notary that is interdicted and not the simple possession of his civil status, least of all when the function of this status is called into play with comparative infrequency, and then only with intimate relation to the needs of the diocesan curia itself.

ARTICLE IV. PENALTIES FOR THE ABUSE OF THE POWERS OF THE CHANCELLOR

The misuse or abuse of the power and duties of the office of chancellor with regard to the proper drawing up and sedulous care of the curial documents can eventuate in a grave delict which calls for the application of severe penalties as enacted in the Code. In general, these penalties are of an indeterminate nature. Their application is left to the prudent judgment of the bishop and they are therefore only *ferendae sententiae* penalties.

All those who forge, counterfeit or falsify any ecclesiastical letters or acts either of a public or of a private nature, or who knowingly make use of them, are to be punished according to the gravity of their fault.[78] These delicts are more grave when they are committed by the person who by his office has these documents or papers in his keeping,[79] as is the case with the chancellor.

In particular, if the chancellor presumptuously falsifies, vitiates, destroys or conceals the curial documents of which he is custodian by virtue of his office, he is to be deprived of his office and he is likewise to be punished by the bishop with other grave penalties proportionate to the gravity of the delinquency.[80] Or again, if the chancellor, who is bound to draw up documents and make copies of the written acts under his care for those who legitimately petition them,[81] either maliciously refuses to draw up such documents or to furnish transcribed copies, or mutilates the documents and books under his care, he may be deprived of his office or suspended by the Ordinary and a fine may be imposed upon him according to the gravity of the case.[82] These abuses of the powers of the chancellor seem to be even more grave when perpetrated during the vacancy of the see, for the reason that the

[78] Can. 2362.
[79] Can. 2404.
[80] Can. 2406, § 1.
[81] Cf. Can. 384, § 1.
[82] Can. 2406, § 2.

Code stresses with a special insistence the seriousness of the care of the curial documents at this time, and absolutely prohibits the making of any withdrawals from the episcopal curia or the effecting of any changes in the documents.[83] The punishment therefore should be more severe for any such delinquency in the misuse of the documents of the curia during the vacancy of the see.

The Code permits bishops and their officials to charge a moderate fee to cover the chancery expenses incurred in connection with the granting of matrimonial dispensations[84] and allows the bishops of the province to fix a certain tax for the execution of rescripts received from the Holy See as well as for the ministration of jurisdictional acts of a non-judicial character.[85] If the chancellor himself increases the rate of these lawfully permitted taxes, or if he exacts more than is allowed in a particular case, he commits a delict for which he should be punished, and he becomes liable even to the paying of a fine as ordered at the discretion of the Ordinary. If he still continues to exact more than is lawful, the Ordinary may suspend him from the exercise of his office or even remove him from his office, according to the degree of guilt present in the offense. Moreover, the chancellor must restore what he has unjustly overcharged.[86]

The presence of these penalties in the law is of significant importance, for the enacted sanctions help to safeguard the ecclesiastical system of legal proof through authentic documents. The very nature of the legal

---

[83] Can. 435, § 3.
[84] Can. 1056.
[85] Can. 1507, § 1.
[86] Can. 2408.

trust and authority reposed in the office of chancellor demands that any misuse of the power of his office by the chancellor be severely punished. If the grave neglect of his duties or the deliberate abuse of his office were not corrected by means of the sanctions enacted in the law, then there would emerge a danger against the public good. In the case wherein such an abuse would be allowed to continue, the character of trustworthiness so essential to the functions of notary and custodian of the archives could no longer be regarded as attaching in fact to the office of the chancellor. This would tend to undermine, at least in that diocese wherein the chancellor holds office, the general legal system of the Church whereby letters, documents or copies of them which are drawn up and signed by the chancellor, are to be accepted as furnishing full proof for the ecclesiastical forum.

CHAPTER VI

The Chancellor as Delegate of the Bishop

Article I. The Habitual Use of the Chancellor as Delegate

In the United States the diocesan chancellor has become a person of notable dignity. This attitude seems to be due to the fact of the chancellor's importance as a delegate of the bishop. It is of common knowledge that ordinarily the chancellor is delegated for the exercise of many of the powers of the Ordinary. This delegation is not given him by the Code, for the general law defines his duty in the diocesan administration only as that of archivist-notary. The power which the chancellor possesses outside of this sphere of duties comes to him, not *a iure,* but *ab homine,* that is, through a mandate of the Ordinary. It is to be further noted that when these powers are delegated to him they do not belong to the office of chancellor as such, but are delegated to the person of the priest who, at the same time, happens to be the incumbent of that office.

That the bishop can grant these powers by way of delegation either in whole or in part is clearly evident from the general law on the matter of delegation.[1] The question for discussion in this article is not concerned with the possibility of the delegating of a priest to act for

[1] "Qui iurisdictionis potestatem habet ordinariam, potest eam alteri ex toto vel ex parte delegare, nisi aliud expresse iure caveatur"—Canon 199, § 1.

the Ordinary in certain matters. Rather, it inquires whether the practice of habitually employing the priest who is the chancellor for the continual and universal exercise of delegated jurisdiction is contrary to the spirit of the Code.

Apart from all effort to explore the concept of delegation as such, it is nevertheless in place to mention a few points about delegation, in view of this present discussion about the practice of granting delegated power to the chancellor.

The delegation of power connotes a human act. Consequently any such act of delegation can be nullified by those factors which vitiate the natural act itself in its capacity of a human act. Such factors include absolute violence, substantial error and antecedent ignorance. But above all, an act of delegation is a juridical act and hence is governed by the provision of the positive law.[2]

Practical necessity is the fundamental basis for granting delegation. When the delegation is *ab homine* this necessity is determined by the difficulty of exercising jurisdiction on the part of one and the same person who is constituted in ordinary power. Such a difficulty can arise from the peculiar circumstances of the place, from the pressure of a multiplicity of activities, or again, from some moral or physical impediment.[3]

Though canon 199 states that ordinary power can be delegated *ex toto,* this does not mean that it can be done in such a way as to imply practically the abdication of

---

[2] Cf. Kearney, *The Principles of Delegation,* The Catholic University of America Canon Law Studies, n. 55 (Washington, D. C.: The Catholic University of America, 1929), p. 75.

[3] Crisci, "De delegatione a iure in iure canonico vigenti,"—Apollinaris, X (1937), 513-535, esp. p. 514.

the ordinary powers nor again that the Ordinary can unburden himself of all his duties.[4] Excessive and imprudent delegations, though not to be considered as invalid, are illicit.[5]

When granting a mandate for delegation the Ordinary should be specific for there is no place for vagueness in the law. In other words, he should state whether his authority is granted for a certain time, for a certain species of acts, or for a definite act only. The fact that the Ordinary should be clear in his mandate is evident. Such clearness is demanded in order that the delegate may know the limits of his power. Without this knowledge the delegate could scarcely proceed to act, for fear that he would be exceeding the limits of his power and in so doing would at the same time be acting invalidly.[6]

From these principles, then, it is evident that if the Ordinary wishes to delegate his power of jurisdiction to the chancellor, natural equity demands: (1) that the fundamental basis for delegating his authority be present in so far as a practical necessity demands this delegation in view of some difficulty in personally exercising his authority; (2) that the Ordinary do not delegate his jurisdiction in such a way as to unburden himself of all jurisdictional duties, and that the delegation of jurisdictional powers be not excessive or imprudent; and (3) that the limits of the power delegated to the chancellor be precisely defined in the mandate of jurisdiction.

Now, relative to the practice of delegating authority to the chancellor, the question may be asked: To what ex-

---

[4] Kearney, *op. cit.*, p. 77.

[5] C. 3, 28, X, *de officio et potestate iudicis delegati*, I, 29.

[6] Can. 203, § 1.

tent may the bishop grant his jurisdictional powers to the chancellor?

It is evident from canon 199 that the Ordinary does have the power of giving delegated jurisdiction to the priest who holds this office, and nothing can be said against the practice of employing the chancellor rather than another priest. It is evidently more convenient that the chancellor be employed as delegate of the bishop, for from the nature of his office he is more often present at the episcopal curia. Whenever the Ordinary himself cannot attend to certain matters, either because of the multitude of affairs or because of his necessary absence, it is a convenient arrangement to delegate the chancellor who is always at hand. The question then narrows down to this; namely, Is it a juridically correct practice for the bishop to grant to his chancellor habitual and general powers of delegation to be fully and continually exercised after the manner of a vicar delegate?[7]

If there existed anywhere the practice of granting such powers to the chancellor, one could of course raise little, if any, doubt about the validity of the granted delegation, for by virtue of canon 199 the bishop must be recognized as being able to delegate his ordinary powers in their entirety. Furthermore, the law nowhere presents any text which either expressly or in some equivalent fashion, according to the norm of canon 11, invokes any sanction of invalidity against such an act of habitual general delegation. But as a question of policy,

[7] A vicar delegate is a priest who takes the place of a vicar general in mission territories that are ruled by a vicar or prefect apostolic. He receives full jurisdiction from his Ordinary as a *delegate* and thus differs from the vicar general in a diocese who has *ordinary* jurisdiction as deriving from the office which he holds.—Cf. *AAS*, XII (1920), 120.

such a practice is contrary to the spirit and intent of the law. This appears certain because of the reasons here subjoined.

To grant to the chancellor such wide powers of delegated authority that he will practically administer most of the spiritual and material rule of the diocese and actually issue most if not all of the dispensations himself, so that the bishop's diocesan jurisdiction is exercised in the main not through *ordinary* power but rather through the chancellor's *delegated* power, is in effect to place the chancellor in the position of a vicar delegate of the bishop. Under such circumstances the chancellor would be exercising, in the same sense as a vicar delegate in mission districts, the full sphere of his bishop's ordinary powers through the latter's act of universal delegation. But the Holy See has defined that the vicar delegate exercises by way of delegation such jurisdictional functions as the vicar general exercises by ordinary jurisdiction where the diocese is established. The office of vicar delegate is set up in mission territory *in place of* the office of vicar general of the diocese.[8] In other words, the vicar delegate is to be appointed only in such places and under such conditions for which the law does not recognize the possible appointment of a vicar general, that is, in mission territories which are ruled by vicars or prefects apostolic. He exists there *instead of* a vicar general. By inference one must conclude that he cannot, in agreement with this provision of the law, exist in a diocese *alongside of* a vicar general, for thus he would acquire by delegated authority the very functions which the law intends to

---

[8] S. C. de Prop. Fide, ep., 8 dec. 1919—*AAS,* XII (1919), 120.

belong to the vicar general, who is to exercise them through ordinary power.

If the chancellor were in fact to exercise so much delegated jurisdiction that he could be considered as a vicar delegate of the bishop, this would evidently do away with much, if not most or even all of the exercise of ordinary authority through the vicar general. It would be a practice contrary to the spirit of the law, which provides for the aid of the bishop in the jurisdictional rule of his diocese through an office to which belongs *ordinary* jurisdiction, namely that of the vicar general, and not through a vicar who exercises delegated power. This practice, if it were continued, would surely tend to leave to the vicar general little else than an office only, since the powers of his office would at the most be seldom called into use. In actuality the position of the vicar general would simply become one of honor next to that of the bishop, but would cease, at least in fact, to be one of jurisdiction concurrent with that of the bishop. In places where such a trend exists this very result is noticeable. The Code does not contemplate any situation in which the vicar general exercises less jurisdiction over the diocese than does the chancellor or another priest. Quite manifestly, then, any practice that leads to such a result cannot be regarded as harmonizing with the spirit of the law.

This practice of authorizing some priest of the diocese to act after the manner of a vicar delegate and thus to supplant the vicar general in his jurisdictional competence seems to obtain in some Spanish speaking countries.[9]

[9] Cf. Ferreres, *Institutiones Canonicae* (2 vols., Barcinone, 1920), I, 674, footnote; Muniz, *Procedimientos Eclesiasticos* (2. ed. 3 vols., Sevilla: Lib. de Sobrino de Izquiedo [no date]), I, 136.

But there, instead of the chancellor of the diocese, it is rather the secretary of the bishop who exercises this widely delegated jurisdiction. In commenting on this condition Wernz-Vidal admit that the practice is alien to the discipline of the Code and that it ought to be corrected.[10]

Even if the chancellor is not considered as a vicar delegate of the bishop, the practice of granting him full delegated authority to be generally and continually exercised in the rule of the diocese still is a policy which is alien to the discipline of the Code. The law has already provided a legally constituted office, the incumbent of which is to help the bishop in the rule of his diocese. Through the institution of the office of vicar general to which is appointed a priest as an *altera persona cum episcopo,* the Code has made provision for filling the very need which manifestly has arisen in those places wherein exists the practice of granting widely delegated habitual powers to the chancellor. If the government of the diocese is beyond the capacity of the bishop alone, the Code orders him to constitute a vicar general who is to lend his aid throughout the entire diocese by means of ordinary power.[11]

This power of the vicar general is meant to be actively employed and is evidently not to be supplanted by the

---

[10] "In multis curiis ecclesiasticis loco cancellarii existit Secretarius Episcopi, cui multa munera sunt commissa, quae proprie pertinent ad Vicarium Generalem. Qui modus a disciplina Codicis est alienus et facile per convenientem immutationem esset reformandus"—Wernz-Vidal, *Ius Canonicum,* II (*De personis*), 690.

[11] "Quoties rectum dioecesis regimen id exigat, constituendus est ab Episcopo Vicarius Generalis, qui ipsum potestate ordinaria in toto territorio adiuvet"—Can. 366, § 1.

exercise of delegated power through the chancellor. The means desired by the Code for the regularly constituted help to the bishop in the exercise of his diocesan rule is one of *ordinary* and *not* one of delegated jurisdiction. Even though canon 199 makes possible the delegation of the Ordinary's power *ex toto,* it can certainly not be argued that such a possible universal delegation is to be understood in the sense of being a normal means made available by the law with a view to providing an habitual aid for the rule of the diocese; an aid which can be invoked only at the cost of supplanting much if not practically all of the exercise of jurisdiction on the part of the vicar general. If the vicar general is thus practically barred from the exercise of his official powers in view of the chancellor's universal delegation, then indeed there is, *de facto,* placed in the hands of the chancellor the power which the Code reposes in the hands of the vicar general. In a word, the *vicarius* rule in the diocese which should reflect the exercise of a *vicarius* ordinary power is then suppressed to an exercise of authority by a mere delegate. It need hardly be reiterated that such a condition of affairs is not in harmony with the purpose of the general law which professedly looks to the office of the vicar general as the medium whence the bishop is to derive his needed help in the government of the diocese.

The practice of making the chancellor the bishop's plenipotentiary delegate militates against the very concept of the office of chancellor as delineated in the Code. The law seems to consider his duties of caring for the documents in the archives and of being the curial notary as a sufficient burden for the full-time attention of the chancellor, otherwise there would hardly be any justified need of the provision of the law which indicates the possible appointment of a vice-chancellor to help him in his work.[12] The very use of the term *cancellarius* in the law connotes only a function that deals with the drawing up and the taking care of documents, and not with the exercise of delegated power for the government of the diocese.[13] It cannot be legitimately argued that the Code has made possible the appointment of a vice-chancellor for the actual work connected with the care of the documents, thus leaving the chancellor himself more free for the exercise of other duties, for the law makes no distinction; both the chancellor and the vice-chancellor have the same duties in the care of documents. To interpret the law on the duties of the chancellor in canon 372 otherwise would not be in harmony with the legal provision for the interpretation of laws according to the proper signification of the words in the law.[14] When it becomes necessary to use the chancellor for the exercise of delegated powers, it seems more in accordance with the spirit of the law not to speak of him as "chancellor" in this particular function, but rather to call him by some other term, such as the "bishop's delegate." Otherwise the term "chancellor" if it be habitually used in designation of the priest who exercises the delegated powers of the bishop, will come to signify a position not foreseen by the Code when it provided that his principal work consisted in the duties of an archivist-notary.

---

[12] Can. 372, § 2.

[13] In the footnotes of canon 372 on the duties of the chancellor, reference is made to the sources of this law. These sources deal only with the care of documents and not with the exercise of delegated powers.

[14] Can. 18.

To argue that the practice of habitually delegating the chancellor for the exercise of general delegation, is a legitimate custom having the force of law would be a valid argument if it could be proved that it is a legal custom. But this can not be proved.

This practice, since it is not according to the law, could only have become a legally binding custom through a continuation of its employment either *praeter* or *contra legem.* But it could not be a legal custom *praeter legem,* since it is evident that the bishop is not bound to follow the practice of employing his chancellor as his delegate whenever he wishes to grant his power to another.[15] Nor can it be considered as a legal custom *contra legem.* Since the advent of the Code there has not been sufficient time for a custom either outside of or contrary to the law to receive binding force.[16] And at the time of the promulgation of the Code it could not have been accepted as an immemorial custom still binding,[17] because a custom can have the force of law only with the consent of the competent superior,[18] which consent was lacking, as is evidenced from a reply of the Holy See to a bishop of the United States in 1896, when he asked for authorization to delegate certain powers to the chancellor.[19] In this private reply the Holy See indirectly disapproved of

---

[15] "Consuetudo praeter legem, quae scienter a communitate cum animo se obligandi servata sit, legem inducit . . ."—Can. 28.

[16] ". . . per annos quadraginta continuos et completos praescripta."—Can. 27.

[17] Can. 5.

[18] Can. 25.

[19] S. C. Prop. Fide, 22 dec. 1896, to the Bishop of Pittsburgh—in *Analecta Ecclesiastica,* VI (1898), p. 10; cf. *Le Canoniste Contemporain,* XXI (1898), 181.

granting delegated powers to the chancellor. It therefore appears unjustified to argue that the practice of granting delegated powers to the chancellor is a custom *having the force of law.* The most that could be said for the practice is that it is a customary convenient arrangement that may be tolerated under certain circumstances.

The mind of the Holy See on the question of granting habitual delegation to the chancellor is not found expressed, outside of the Code, in any published document except in the private reply just mentioned. Perhaps it is the only occasion on which any published correspondence with Rome mentions this subject under discussion. Since the reply from Rome seems to indicate that the Sacred Congregation was not in favor of the idea of granting delegation to the chancellor, it will be of some profit to examine the reply more closely.

The Bishop of Pittsburgh had asked for permission to subdelegate to the chancellor certain matrimonial faculties which he had received and could already grant to his vicar general. He had given as a reason the fact that the vicar general resided in another city away from the bishop, but that the chancellor was at hand in the bishop's curia.[20] In reply the Sacred Congregation ignored the idea of subdelegating the chancellor. It told the bishop to appoint in the city where the bishop resided, another vicar general through whom these faculties could be exercised.[21] Even though the Congregation

[20] ". . . ut infrascripto concedere dignetur potestatem subdelegandi Cancellario Episcopali, qui secum in domo residet, easdem facultates aeque ac Vicario Generali."—*Analecta Ecclesiastica,* VI (1898), 10; *Le Canoniste Contemporain,* XXI (1898), 181.

[21] "Per duas epistolas in mense novembri . . . petebat facultatem subdelegandi easdem facultates etiam cancellario residenti in Curia, si Vicarius

permitted the faculties in question to be delegated to an ordinary priest in the outlying districts of the diocese,[22] it appeared to object precisely to the fact of granting these faculties to the chancellor, and asked instead that a priest be nominated from the city as a vicar general.[23] The meaning was evident. If the bishop wished to have the chancellor or any priest in the Curia to exercise these faculties, he could do so by appointing him in the capacity of a second vicar general in the diocese.

ARTICLE II. THE OCCASIONAL USE OF THE CHANCELLOR AS DELEGATE

Though it has been shown that to provide for the continuous exercise of the jurisdiction of the Ordinary through the delegation of habitual powers to the chancellor is contrary to the purpose and intent of the Code of Canon Law, this nevertheless does not mean that the convenient usage of employing the chancellor as an *occasional* delegate of the bishop, as is frequently done in the United States, is alien to the law. For, as it has been pointed out, canon 199 gives the bishop the authority to delegate his power, and since it is not expressly for-

---

Generalis non ibi resideat . . . Si igitur Amplitudo Tua difficilem putat esse accessum ad Vicarium Generalem si alibi resideat, et opportunius esse ut facultates habeat aliquis qui degat in Curia, potest uni alterive sacerdoti in remotioribus dioecesis partibus degenti facultates delegari ad normam formulae, et alium sacerdotem in urbe residentiali habitantem Vicarium suum Generalem nominare cui soli inter Vicarios eiusmodi poterunt dictae facultates subdelegari."—*Loc. cit.*

[22] "Potest uni alterive sacerdote in remotioribus dioecesis partibus degenti facultates delegari . . ."—*Loc. cit.*

[23] "Si Amplitudo putat . . . opportunius esse ut facultates habeat aliquis qui degat in Curia, potest . . . sacerdotem in urbe residentiali habitantem, Vicarium suum Generalem nominare."—*Loc. cit.*

bidden for the chancellor to act as an occasional delegate, the Ordinary can certainly so employ the priest in this office. It can not be denied that the convenience of this office being in the curia, bringing an association of close contact between the chancellor and the Ordinary, affords a logical reason for the selection of the chancellor as an occasional delegate when the bishop and vicar general are to be absent. Since the chancellor is the one who generally draws up the document for the issuing of the dispensation, it is simply a rule of convenience that to him also be given the delegated power of granting the dispensation when some one or other has to be delegated because of the absence of the Ordinaries. As long as the chancellor's possession of such delegated power connotes but an occasional or temporary grant which is entrusted to him in such a way as not to discredit in practice the need of a vicar general, the use of this procedure in itself is not contrary to the spirit of the law. However, it is of common knowledge that very often in the chanceries where the chancellor is employed as the one through whom dispensations are granted by delegated power, it becomes an habitual practice so to employ him instead of the vicar general. Under such circumstances the vicar general is not afforded the opportunity to function fully in accordance with the law as far as the *actual* exercise of his jurisdiction is concerned. Therefore it seems to be more according to the wish of the Code if the bishop will only sparingly employ as his delegate, the priest who holds the office of chancellor, in order that he will not infringe upon the concurrent exercise of diocesan jurisdiction through the ordinary channel of the vicar general, which office has been established by law as the medium through which the bishop will derive his needed help in his administrative government of the diocese.

The same norm seems to hold also relative to the exercise of other powers in the administration of the rule of the diocese besides the issuing of dispensations. If to the chancellor is delegated the responsibility of property administration in the diocese, or the duty of receiving and arbitrating the complaints of the clergy and the laity in minor matters, or the authority of deciding as chancellor whether or not certain petitions have sufficient merits to be brought to the attention of the diocesan tribunal, or the performance of other like functions of diocesan administration which by general law do not belong to the office of chancellor, such a practice seems alien to the mind of the legislator as reflected in the discipline of the Code. For in such a practice there is a supplanting of the exercise of an *ordinary* jurisdiction, which is to be supplied through a vicar general and an *officialis* (when the bishop can not personally attend to these matters) by the application of a *delegated* jurisdictional rule. It would gradually lead to an understanding in the diocese that the chancellor, *qua chancellor,* holds an office through which much of the ruling of the diocese is done, and there would be attributed to the office itself an honor and a function that is evidently not intended by the law. For it would become altogether apparent that the chancellor does not simply act as a delegate of the bishop on occasion, rather it would appear that the bishop has set up a new office to which attaches the permanent exercise of his delegated powers. This condition seems to exist *de facto* in many parts of the United States and Canada.

This is evident from the important position which attaches to the chancellor in those places.[24]

But can not the bishop constitute a new office, it may be argued, or could he not make an innovation in the office of chancellor by giving to him, *qua chancellor,* an exercise of jurisdiction in the administration of the diocese?

According to Maroto,[25] although an ecclesiastical office must, in virtue of canon 145, be instituted *by law,* it is not necessary that this be the *general* law. Sometimes an office may receive its institution through a particular legislation, for instance, a diocesan law. Thus the Ordinary who has legislative power in his own territory, has the requisite capacity to institute by a diocesan law some office that is unrecognized in the general or particular law, and also to determine its rights and obligations. This is only for his own diocese. Maroto however states that this competency of the bishop extends only to some kind of minor office,[26] However true this may be, it is not directly significant for the question in hand. For if the bishop keeps the office of chancellor but at the same time attaches to this office functions not specified in the law, then it is not the question of the institution of a

---

[24] "In the United States the diocesan chancellor has become a unique personage of distinction, influence, power and administrative responsibility." —Doheny, *Canonical Procedure in Matrimonial Cases* (Milwaukee: Bruce, 1938), p. 54.

[25] *Institutiones Iuris Canonici,* I, p. 679, n. 582.

[26] ". . . item a iure particulari, imprimis dioecesano, possunt esse instituta in genere nonnulla officia ecclesiastica, quae deinde numerice ab homine erigantur; denique nihil impedit quominus. . . . Ordinarius valeat aliquando instituere in casu particulari officium aliquod in iure tam generali quam particulari incognitum, eiusque iura et obligationes determinare; . . . Ordinarii sunt competentes generatim ad officia minora, salvis limitationibus . . ."—Maroto, *loc. cit.*

new office, but rather of an *innovation* in an office that is already established by the general law. By this *innovation* in an ecclesiastical office is understood some change from the state that it had originally in the law. This change may be reflected either in regard to the temporal or spiritual rights and obligations, or in regard to its localized see, its territorial extension, or its specific character.[27]

And so it may be asked, can the bishop make such an innovation in the office held by the chancellor that *to his office* there will thenceforth attach the right of exercising some jurisdiction in the administration of the diocese, a jurisdiction that is over and above the right of exercising authority as an archivist-notary, which right is the only one enacted in the general law as pertaining to the office of chancellor?

If the bishop were to do so, then the power of jurisdiction which the chancellor would obtain through his office would have to be either an ordinary or a delegated power. But since delegated power is defined as that which is granted to a person,[28] the attached power as inherent in the office, could not be of a *delegated* character. On the other hand, since ordinary power is defined as that which *by law* is annexed to an office,[29] the bishop must have to effect this annexation of power to the office by means of a diocesan law before it could enjoy the status of *ordinary* power. But such a procedure would imply a disregard

---

[27] Maroto, *op. cit.* I, 678.

[28] "Potestas iurisdictionis . . . delegata, quae commissa est personae"—Can. 197.

[29] "Potestas iurisdictionis ordinaria ea est quae ipso iure adnexa est officio"—Can. 197.

of the discipline of the Code inasmuch as the Code has established the office of vicar general, which enjoys ordinary power, for the purpose which the bishop by such a procedure would want to serve. In place of such an innovation relative to the office of chancellor, the bishop could readily appoint another vicar general if the extent of the diocese or the multiplicity of administrative duties demanded more help than the one vicar general could lend. The law itself in canon 366 allows this.

Thus the practice of employing the chancellor as a plenipotentiary episcopal delegate in the exercise of diocesan administration, or even the possible attempt to grant this jurisdiction to the office as such, appears altogether alien to, if not also in absolute disharmony with, the discipline of the Code. From this conclusion there seems to be no escape.

ARTICLE III. SOME PARTICULAR QUESTIONS ON THE USE OF CERTAIN DELEGATED POWERS THROUGH THE CHANCELLOR

The preceding articles have shown that the granting of the power of habitual delegation to the chancellor or the attempt to attach ordinary jurisdiction for ruling the diocese to his office as such militates against the discipline of the Code. Nevertheless it must be again remarked that, since canon 199 permits the delegation of ordinary jurisdiction, and since necessity often demands that this be done for the better administration of the diocese when for various reasons the Ordinary is not at hand, practical convenience seems to demand that the priest who is the chancellor is also the one who should be employed for the occasional exercise of such delegated jurisdiction. He is most generally at hand because of the nature of his duties in the diocesan curia. Inasmuch as it is a common practice in the United States occasionally to delegate extensive powers to the chancellor, it is the purpose of the present article to discuss a few practical questions that may arise with regard to the actual exercise of some of the delegated faculties granted to the priest who is at the same time the diocesan chancellor. For instance, can the chancellor subdelegate his own delegated power to dispense in some cases of matrimonial impediments, or can he as a bishop's delegate designate others to assist at marriage?

According to canon 199, § 2, the bishop has the power to subdelegate the delegated powers which he has received from the Holy See. He may grant this subdelegation either for a single act or for a habitual exercise, except in the case that the Holy See has selected him as its delegate in view of a personal qualification, or when subdelegation has been prohibited.[30]

Now, among the delegated powers in the faculties received from the Holy See which can be habitually delegated are the faculties to dispense from the matrimonial impediments of mixed religion and of disparity of worship.[31] The bishop then can validly give these faculties to his chancellor, so that this priest in turn can habitually

---

[30] "Etiam potestas iurisdictionis ab Apostolica Sede delegata subdelegare potest sive ad actum, sive habitualiter, nisi electa fuerit industria personae aut subdelegatio prohibita."

[31] An English translation of the rescript of the quinquennial faculties (Formula IV) granted to the bishops of the United States in 1939, is given in Bouscaren, *Canon Law Digest*, supplement, 1941, pp. 26-38.

grant these dispensations by his own subdelegated authority, with the understanding of course that the conditions necessary for granting them be realized.

1. But here a question may arise. Can the chancellor in turn, delegate these faculties even for a single case to another priest for the granting of a dispensation of this kind? This can not be done, for the chancellor is already exercising in this case a *subdelegated* power of the Holy See as deriving from his local Ordinary. Without an express concession he can not again subdelegate this power to another even for a single case.[32] Therefore in practice, it will not be a valid act if the chancellor, even though he have an habitual subdelegated power, grants to the vice-chancellor or any other priest the power to dispense from the impediment of disparity of worship or of mixed religion if, for example, he has to be away from the chancery office when a petition for such a dispensation arrives. The reason for which he may consider that he has such a power may possibly arise from a misunderstanding of the third paragraph of canon 199, which speaks of *delegated* power for a universal number of cases by one who, as an intermediate to the Holy Father, possesses ordinary power, then such a *delegated* power can in turn be subdelegated in individual cases.[33] The law reads "delegated" and not "subdelegated" power. The difficulty arises from the fact that since the chancellor in other things is often the *delegate* of the bishop,

---

[32] "Nulla potestas subdelegata potest iterum subdelegari nisi id expresse concessum fuit"—Can. 199, § 5.

[33] "Potestas *delegata* ad universitatem negotiorum ab eo qui infra Romanum Pontificum habet ordinariam potestatem, potest in singulis casibus subdelegari."

he might also consider himself as a delegate of the bishop in exercising the faculties which he has received through the bishop from the Holy See. In reality he is only a *subdelegate*. In this case he has no delegated power, and consequently can not apply canon 199, § 3, in order to subdelegate that power in individual cases, even though he himself has a subdelegated power which he may use quite comprehensively, and even though in other things he may simultaneously possess a delegated power which derives from the bishop's ordinary jurisdiction. Therefore a dispensation from the impediment of mixed religion or disparity of worship granted by a priest or a vice-chancellor by authority of the chancellor is invalid, unless the permission to grant such a further subdelegation has been expressly conceded by the Holy See.[34]

2. There are other faculties which are granted by the Holy See to the bishop himself. These are to be exercised personally by the Ordinary and can not be subdelegated to the chancellor. One of these faculties, for example, is the power of granting a *sanatio in radice* for a marriage attempted before a minister or civil officer when an impediment of mixed religion or disparity of worship exists.[35]

There are two methods open to the Ordinary in the exercising of this faculty personally: Either he may himself directly concede this favor, or he may commit another priest, such as the chancellor, to execute this favor in *forma commissoria*. According to canon 54 the execution of a rescript according to the *forma commis-*

---

[34] "Nulla subdelegata potestas potest iterum subdelegari, nisi id expresse concessum fuerit"—Can. 199, § 5; cf. also § 4.

[35] Bouscaren, *op. cit.*, p. 28.

soria can be committed to a minister in two ways. Either the chancellor (or any other priest) is employed as a mere minister (*nudum ministerium*) with no choice but to grant the favor as a simple executor (*in forma commissoria necessaria*), or the chancellor is commissioned in such a manner that he may grant it or deny it as he wills (*in forma commissoria voluntaria*).[36]

Now the question arises: Even though the Ordinary is not enabled to subdelegate this faculty to his chancellor, could he not communicate it in *forma commissoria voluntaria?* In other words, could the bishop commit to the chancellor the execution of a rescript in which he grants the sanation, dependent on the judgment of the chancellor himself whether or not it should be granted, even when the conditions necessary for the sanation are present? The bishop could not do this validly because he would be making the chancellor actually a voluntary executor, and a voluntary executor of a rescript is truly acting simply as a delegate.[37] Since the bishop is prohibited in the proposed case from subdelegating his power, he is also prohibited from entrusting the *voluntary* execution of it to his chancellor, for thus the chancellor would actually be constituted as the bishop's subdelegate.

Therefore if the bishop wishes to employ his chancellor in the granting of this sanation but at the same time desires to act personally as the faculty demands, he may

---

[36] Cf. Maroto, *Institutiones Iuris Canonici,* I, p. 310, n. 278, sub littera "c"; Cappello, *De sacramentis,* III (*De matrimonio,* Romae, 1933), n. 280.

[37] "Executor voluntarius, qui melius vocaretur delegatus, est ille, cui tributur potius facultas exequendi, seu committitur ipsa concessio gratiae"—Maroto, *op. cit.,* I, p. 331, n. 288; cf. Vromant, *Ius Missionariorum,* V (*De matrimonio,* Louvain, 1931), 107.

employ the chancellor only as a *necessary* executor or as a simple agent to carry out the bishop's already determined wish. In other words, the bishop grants the rescript to the parties directly, but provides that it will have its effect only when the chancellor executes it after having ascertained that the necessary conditions are fulfilled. The chancellor can not deny the bestowed favor once the essential conditions are fulfilled.[38]

A somewhat parallel procedure may be validly used by the bishop should he wish to grant certain extraordinary faculties, which he has as delegate of the Holy See, to certain priests through the ministry of the chancellor, without making the chancellor a subdelegate. He may validly proceed in this manner: The bishop delegates his power of appointing, say, parochial assistants or perhaps chaplains, to his chancellor. Then he subdelegates directly the extraordinary faculties he has received from the Holy See to the parochial assistants or chaplains, as the case may be, at that moment in which the chancellor actually appoints them. In this procedure the chancellor acts only as a necessary executor of the will of the bishop in the granting of the faculties, even though he acts as a true delegate of the bishop in the appointing of the assistants or the chaplains. The will of the chancellor never enters into the action of the passing of the faculties to these priests; his will enters only into the action of appointing them to the position in which, by their very appointment, they immediately receive the extraordinary faculties from the bishop. In this matter of the faculties, the chancellor acts as a mere executor or

[38] C. Cappello, *op. cit.*, n. 280; Vromant, *op. cit.*, p. 107.

minister. However, were the bishop to recognize the right of the chancellor to withhold for any reason whatsoever the granting of the faculties even when the assistant or chaplain has been appointed, then the chancellor will no longer be a mere minister, but an actual subdelegate of the Holy See. Further subdelegation beyond the chancellor would in this case be invalid, unless this were expressly permitted by the Holy See.

A procedure more in harmony with the spirit of the Code is to employ the vicar general in place of the chancellor, for in this case there would be invested the same power in the vicar general as in the bishop. As *altera persona cum episcopo* he is able to exercise faculties given personally to the bishops, unless it is evident that in rare cases the Holy See would employ a bishop in the exercise of a faculty by reason of the bishop's own personal excellence (*industria personae*).

3. In regard to the next point of discussion which treats of the question whether the chancellor as delegate of the bishop can designate others to assist at marriages, the term "delegation" is used for this act of granting permission to assist at marriage as it is also so employed in the Code,[39] though it is acknowledged that a priest who assists as an officially qualified witness does not really exercise jurisdiction in the strict sense.[40]

It may be asked in this connection whether the bishop can delegate to the chancellor his own capacity, which he

---

[39] Canons 1094, 1098.

[40] "Assistentia matrimonio . . . non est actus iurisdictionis . . . nihilominus huiusmodi assistentia habet analogiam cum iurisdictionis, idcirco quae dicuntur de iurisdictione, dicenda quoque sunt aliqua ratione de assistentia"—Cappello, *De Sacramentis*, III (*De matrimonio*), n. 670, n. 672.

himself has by ordinary jurisdiction, of delegating priests for assistance at marriages, so that the chancellor can himself appoint a determinate priest to assist at a determinate marriage according to canon 1096, § 1. The Ordinary has the power from canon 1094 both to assist and to delegate for assistance at marriage. Since this power is *ordinary,* one must naturally assume that the bishop has the ability to delegate *ex toto* to the chancellor unless there be some specific provision which in law forbids this. There are those who, in abstracting from other provisions of law than the general principle of canon 199, § 1, might contend that by delegation of general powers of the Ordinary, the chancellor could both assist and delegate to assist at marriage, whether for a single marriage or for all marriages throughout the diocese. Thus, in canon 1095, § 2, in place of the term "Ordinary," substitute the term "chancellor" as delegate of the bishop. This would accordingly endow the chancellor with a power equivalent to that accorded to the Ordinary. With the possession of this power the chancellor could then proceed to designate a determinate priest for assistance at a determinate marriage according to the rule of canon 1096, § 1, without any further permission for an individual case from the Ordinary.

However this line of argumentation is definitely untenable, and the chancellor is unable to act as the general delegate of the bishop to officially appoint a priest to assist at a marriage. Nor would he himself be able to assist at even one marriage, in his capacity of a general delegate of the bishop.[41]

---

[41] The present discussion prescinds from the fact that the chancellor *as an assistant pastor* could obtain a general delegation to assist at marriages

When canon 199, § 1, by general rule permits ordinary power to be delegated, it adds the qualifying clause, *nisi aliud expresse iure caveatur.* Canon 1096, § 1, reveals such a law whereby the general rule of canon 199, § 1, must yield to the very exception for which it left room. All general delegations to assist at marriage are excluded by law save in the case where this may be given to parochial assistants within the limits of the parish to which they are attached.[42] Thus it is certainly evident that the Ordinary can not grant the chancellor general delegation to assist at marriages throughout the diocese. And if he can not himself assist through this supposed general delegation, then it appears illogical to maintain that he can be given a general power to appoint others to assist. This would be contrary to the philosophical principle of *nemo dat quod non habet* and against the juridical principle of *nemo plus iuris transferre in alium, quam sibi competere dignoscatur.*[43]

Therefore if the chancellor grants to a priest the power to assist at a marriage, without himself being *specially* authorized to subdelegate his own delegation to assist at *that* marriage, or without a general delegation within a certain parish as a parochial assistant, then his grant is certainly invalid, for under such circumstances he lacks

within the parish wherein he is appointed. It further prescinds from the fact that the chancellor could be delegated for assistance at a specific marriage with the faculty of subdelegating some other priest to assist at the same marriage; cf. *Pontificia Commissio Interpretationis,* 28 dec. 1927, ad IV, n. 2—*AAS,* XX (1928), 62.

[42] "Licentia assistendi matrimonio concessa ad normam can. 1095, § 2, dari expresse debet sacerdoti determinato ad matrimonium determinatum, exclusis quibuslibet delegationibus generalibus, nisi agatur de vicariis cooperatoribus pro paroecia cui addicti sunt; secus irrita est"—Can. 1096, § 1.

[43] Reg. 79, R.J., in VI°.

all power, whether as deriving from any precept of the law or as deriving from the ordinary supposed delegation.

An objection might be raised: If the bishop delegated all the powers and faculties of the vicar general to the chancellor or made the chancellor a so-called vicar general *in matrimonialibus* or *in spiritualibus,* could not the chancellor then appoint a priest to assist at marriage, for then he would be able to do all that is in the power of the vicar general to do, which includes this power of delegation? The answer is that this arrangement would make the chancellor no more able to act than if he were a general delegate. For the chancellor would then be either a vicar general with ordinary power, or not a vicar general with only delegated power at the most. The bishop can not delegate to a chancellor the powers of a vicar general and then consider him as an Ordinary. Since the vicar general holds an office, the content of which consists of ordinary jurisdiction, the legal provision of the law must be followed in establishing that office, otherwise the appointment will not be that of a vicar general.[44] Since under this proposed arrangement the chancellor would have the powers of the vicar general only by delegation, the same condition would exist as has already been mentioned: In the event of general delegation of power to the chancellor, he would not be able to appoint any priest for assistance at any marriage, nor would he be able to personally assist at any marriage; in the event of a particular delegation for a particular marriage, he would of course be qualified for valid assistance, but he would not be able to appoint any other priest for

[44] Cf. canons 147, 148 and 366.

this determinate marriage, unless the one who delegated the chancellor for the particular marriage, at the same time expressed the authorization of a further subdelegation.

CONCLUSIONS

1. The term *chancellor* is of ancient origin and was employed as a title for a civil officer who helped the magistrate in the courts of Roman times. This term was sometimes given to the *civil* notaries whom the bishops were empowered to appoint by legislation of Charlemagne. This was in imitation of the nomenclature which attached to the royal chancellor of the king. This nomenclature continued to be used, so that, when under Pope Innocent III there was enacted the first general law ordering *ecclesiastical* notaries by appointment of the bishop in every diocesan curia, these diocesan notaries were at times also termed *chancellors*.

2. Up to the sixteenth century, one finds no ecclesiastical legislation, not even by way of particular law, which directly treats of the office of diocesan chancellor as it is now defined in canon 372.

3. The III Provincial Council of Milan (1575) under St. Charles Borromeo indicates a definite change in the legislation on the diocesan chancellor. For the first time in a particular law his office is defined as it now obtains in the Code of Canon Law.

4. Before the publication of this present Code of Canon Law there was no universally binding law of the Church which defined the office of diocesan chancellor. The development of the present law took place through particular legislation and practical usage. These agencies gradually attributed the name of *chancellor* to the

one who was the notary of the episcopal curia, and specifically to that notary who had care of the safe-keeping of the documents drawn up by all the notaries of the diocese. Thus his two functions, that of notary and that of archivist, are now combined into one office which the universal law defines as the office of diocesan chancellor.

5. The function of the chancellor is truly an ecclesiastical office, for it exists as an institution of law independently of the will of the bishop and connotes at least some participation in jurisdiction through the imposed duty of the administration of the documents of the curia.

6. The practice of treating the office of chancellor as a position in which a priest can be constituted as an habitual general delegate of the Ordinary in the exercise of jurisdiction is a usage that cannot be defended. It is a practice that is contrary to the spirit of the Code, which provides that the diocese should be habitually ruled by means of *ordinary* jurisdiction either of the bishop or of his vicar general. The continuation of the practice tends to do away with the exercise of the functions of the office of vicar general, which office has been established by the general law for the very purpose for which an habitual general delegate is actually employed, namely, for the purpose of furnishing aid to the bishop in the exercise of his jurisdiction. Such a practice tends also to depress the juridical status of a diocese to the level of a vicariate or prefecture apostolic, in which the Ordinary is aided in the exercise of his jurisdiction through the appointment of a vicar delegate *in place of* a vicar general.

7. The chancellor can not, in virtue of his received

general subdelegation of the bishop's own delegated powers, authorize another priest to exercise this jurisdiction even for a particular case (e.g., authorize the vice-chancellor to grant a dispensation from mixed religion or disparity of worship), unless this subdelegation were expressly permitted by the Holy See.

8. In the case where the subdelegation of power is either undesirable or impossible, the chancellor can be made the commissary, as an *executor necessarius,* of a rescript that communicates this power to another or grants a dispensation through the exercise of that power. He can not be the *executor voluntarius* without, at the same time, he become a subdelegate.

9. The chancellor can not in virtue solely of a general delegation *even of all the powers of the Ordinary* assist validly at any marriage. Nor, as a general delegate of the Ordinary, can he validly designate a particular priest to assist at a specific marriage. Unlike parochial assistants the chancellor can not be made the recipient of a general delegation to assist at the marriages of any particular parish, unless he is simultaneously given the legal standing of a parochial assistant.

BIOGRAPHICAL NOTE

John Edward Prince was born on February 21, 1910, at Spokane, Washington. In this same city, after completing his primary education, he attended Gonzaga High School and Gonzaga University, receiving from the latter institution the degree of Bachelor of Arts in 1931. After a year at St. Patrick's Seminary, Menlo Park, California, he entered the North American College and Gregorian University at Rome, Italy, for his theological studies. He was ordained to the priesthood there, on December 8, 1935, and returned to America in 1936. After three years of parish work in the Diocese of Spokane, he enrolled in the School of Canon Law at the Catholic University of America, from which institution he obtained the Baccalaureate in Canon Law in June, 1940, and the Licentiate in Canon Law in June, 1941.

BIBLIOGRAPHY

Sources

Acta Apostolicae Sedis, Commentarium Officiale, Romae, 1909-

Acta et Decreta Concill Plenarii Americae Latinae in Urbe Celabrati, A. D. MDCCCXCIC, Romae, 1902.

Acta et Decreta Concilii Plenarii Baltimorensis Tertii, A. D. MDCCCLXXXIV, Baltimorae: John Murphy, 1886.

Acta et Decreta Sanctorum Conciliorum Recentorum, Collectio Lacensis, 7 vols., Friburgi Brisgoviae, 1870-1890.

Bullarium Diplomatum et Privilegiorum Sanctorum Romanorum Pontificum, Taurinensis editio, 24 vols., and appendix, ed. Francisco Gaudé, Augustae Taurinorum, 1857-1872.

Codex Iuris Canonici Pii X Pontificis Maximi iussu degestus Benedicti XV auctoritate promulgatus, ed. Petri Card. Gasparri, Civitate Vaticana: Typis Polyglottis Vaticanis, 1934.

Codicis Iuris Canonici Fontes cura Emi. Petri Card. Gasparri editi, 9 vols., Romae [later, Civitate Vaticana]: Typis Polyglottis Vaticanis, 1923-1939. (Vols. VII, VIII, IX, *ed. cura et studio Emi. Justiniani Card. Serédi.*)

Corpus Iuris Civilis, edd. Kreuger-Mommsen-Schoell-Kroll, 3 vols., Berolini, 1928-1929.

Decretales D. Gregorii Papae IX una cum Glossa Restitutae, Romae, 1582.

Harduin, Jean, *Acta Conciliorum et Epistolae Decretales ac Constitutiones Summorum Pontificum,* 12 vols., Parisiis, 1715.

Lucanae Ecclesiae Synodus Dioecesana, Lucae, 1887.

Mansi, Joannes, *Sacrorum Conciliorum Nova et Amplissima Collectio,* 53 vols. in 59, Paris, Arnhem, Leilzig, 1901-1927.

Monumenta Germaniae Historica, Auctores Antiquissimi, 15 vols., 1877-1919, Vol. XII, ed. Mommsen, Berolini, 1894.

Momumenta Germaniac Historica, Leges, 5 toms., toms. I, II, III and IV, ed. Georgius Pretz, Hannoverae, 1835-1868, tom. V, ed. Societas aperiedis fontibus rerum germanicarum medii aevi, Hannoverae, 1899.

Monumenta Germaniae Historica, Legum Sectio II, Capitularia Regum Francorum, 2 toms., ed. Alfredus Boretius et Victor Krause, Hannoverae, tom. I, 1890, tom. II, 1897.

Monumenta Germaniae Historica, Legum Section III, Concilia aevi merovingici, tom. I, ed. Fredericus Maassen, Hannoverae, 1893.

Pallottini, Salvator, *Collectio Omnium Conclusionum et Resolutionum Quae in Causis Propositis apud Sacram Congregationem Cardinalium S. Concilium Tridentini Interpretum Prodierunt ab ejus Institutione anno MDLXIV ad MDCCCLX, Distinctis Titulis Alphabetico Ordine per Materias Digestas, 18 vols.,* Romae, 1868-1896.

Quaranta, Stephanus, *Summa Bullarii Eorumve Summorum Pontificum Constitutionum,* Venetiis, 1662.

Ratti, Achille later, Pope Pius XI, *Acta Ecclesiae Mediolanensis ab eius Initiis usque ad Nostram Aetatem,* 3 vols., Mediolani, 1890-1892.

Synodus Dioecesana Ferrariensis, MDCCLXXXI, Ferraris, 1891.

Theodosiani Libri XVI cum Constitutionibus Sirmondianis, ed. Mommsen, Berolini: apud Weidmannos, 1845.

Wilkins, David, *Concilia Magnae Brittaniae et Hiberniae,* 4 vols., Londini, 1737.

Zamboni, Joannes Fortunatus, *Collectio Declarationum Sacrae Congregationis Cardinalium Sacri Concilii Tridentini Interpretum Quae Consentanea ad Tridentinorum Patrum Decreta, easque Canonici Iuris Sanctiones Saeculo XVII in Causis Propositis Prodierunt,* 4 vols., Atrebati, 1860-1868.

Reference Works

Augustine, Charles, *A Commentary on the New Code of Canon Law,* 8 vols., Vol. II, 5. ed., St. Louis: Herder, 1928.

Baart, Peter, *The Legal Formulary,* 2. ed., New York, 1898.

Barbosa, Augustinus, *Summa Apostolicarum Decisionum Extra Ius Commune Vagantium,* Lugduni, 1658.

Benedictus XIV (Prosper Lambertini), *De Synodo Dioecesana,* libri 13 in 2 tom., Lovanii, 1763.

Benson, E. W., *The Cathedral,* London: Murray, 1878.

Blat, Albertus, *Commentarium Textus Codicis Iuris Canonici,* 6 vols., Romae, 1921-1927.

Böuard, *Manuel de diplomatique francaise et pontificale,* Paris: Picard, 1929.

Bouix, *Tractatus de Judiciis Ecclesiasticis,* 2 vols., Parisiis, 1855.

Bouscaren, T. Lincoln, *Canon Law Digest, Officially Published Documents Affecting the Code of Canon Law,* 2 vols. and supplement, Miliwaukee: Bruce, 1934-1941.

Bresslau, Harry, *Handbuch der Urkundenlehre für Deutschland und Italien,* 2. ed., 2 vols., Leipzig, 1912.

Caietanus, Felix V., *Juris Canonici Universi Commentarius* [?], ed., Monachi, 1703.

Chokier, *Commentaria in Regulas Cancellariae Apostolicae,* 3. ed., Coloniae Agrippae, 1674.

Cappello, Felix M., *Praxis Processualis,* Romae: Marietti, 1940.

———, *Tractatus Canonico-Moralis de Sacramentis,* Vol. III, *De matrimonio,* Romae, 1933.

Coronata, Matthaeus, Conte a, *Institutiones Iuris Canonici,* 5 vols., Taurini: Marietti, 1928-1939, vols. I-II, 2. ed., 1939.

D'Angelo, S., *La Curia Diocesana, a norma del Codice di Diritto Canonico,* Giarre (Sicilia): Pietro Lisi, 1922.

De Lugo, Ioannes, *Disputationum de Iustitia et de Iure Libri duo,* 2. ed., 2 vols., Lugduni, 1670.

Doheny, William J., *Canonical Procedure in Matrimonial Cases,* Milwaukee: Bruce, 1938.

Du Cange, Carolus Dufresne, *Glossarium ad Scriptores Mediae et Infimae Latinitatis,* 6 vols., Parisiis, 1733.

Duchesne, Louis, *Le Liber Pontificalis,* 2 vols., Parisiis, 1866.

Fagnanus, Prosper, *Commentarium in Decretalium Libros* [?], ed., Romae, 1661.

Ferraris, F. Lucius, *Prompta Bibliotheca Canonica, Juridica, Moralis, Historica, Theologica necnon Ascetica, Polemica, Rubristica,* 9 vols., Romae, 1885-1899.

Ferreres, Ioannes B., *Institutiones Canonicae,* 2 vols., Barcinone, 1920.

Forcellini, A., et Facciolati, J., *Lexicon Totius Latinitatis,* 5 vols., Pataviae, 1871.

Fournier, Paul, *Les officialités au Moyen-Age,* Paris, 1880.

Giry, *Manuel de diplomatique,* Paris: Hachette, 1894.

Kearney, R. A., *The Principles of Delegation,* The Catholic University of America Canon Law Studies, n. 55, Washington, D. C., 1929.

Lega, M., *De Iudiciis Ecclesiasticis,* 2 vols., Romae, 1896-1898.

Lega, M., Bartoccetti, V., *Commentarius in Iudicia Ecclesiastica,* 3 vols., Romae: Anonima Libreria Catolica Italiana, 1939-1941.

Louis, W. F., *Diocesan Archives,* The Catholic University of America Canon Law Studies, n. 137, Washington, D. C.: The Catholic University of America Press, 1941.

Luchaire, A., *Social France at the time of Philip Augustus* (translated from the 2. ed. by Krehbiel), London: Murray, 1912.

Mangisch, M., *De la Situation et de l'organisation du notariat en Valais,* Saint-Maurice, 1913.

Maroto, Philippus, *Institutiones Iuris Canonici,* 2 vols., Matriti, 1919.

Maupied, Francisco, *Compendium juris canonici,* 2 vols., Parisiis, 1863.

Migne, J. P., *Patrologiae Cursus Completus,* Series Latina, 221 vols., Parisiis, 1844-1864.

Moerner, F., *Dissertatio Academica de Cancellariis,* Upsaliae, 1790.

Mommsen, T., *Gesammelte Schriften,* 6 vols., Berlin, 1910.

Moore, *The Works of Peter of Poitiers,* Washington, D. C.: The Catholic University of America Press, 1936.

Morel, Octave, *La grande chancellerie royale et l'expédition des lettres royaux,* Paris: Picard, 1900.

Moroni, Gaetano, *Dizionario di Erudizione Storico-Ecclesiastica,* 103 vols., plus 6 vols. of index, Venezia, 1840-1879.

Muniz, T., *Procedimientos Eclesiásticos,* 2. ed., 3 vols., Sevilla: Lib. de Sobrino de Izquiedo [no date].

Murray, *A New English Dictionary on Historical Principles,* Oxford, 1893.

Ojetti, B., *Commentarium in Codicem Iuris Canonicis,* 4 vols., Romae, 1927-1931.

Pauly, August F., *Real-Encyclopaedie der classischen Altertumswissenschaft; Neue Bearbeitung, unter Mitwirkung zahlreicher Fachgenossen, herausgeben von Wissowa, Kroll, und Mittelhaus,* 38 vols. and 6 supplements in 58 toms., Stuttgart, 1894-1938.

Pignatelli, Jacobus, *Consultationes Canonicae,* 11 vols. in 4 toms., Coloniae Allobrogum, 1700.

Prümmer, Dominicus, *Manuale Iuris Canonici,* 4. ed., Friburgi Brisgoviae: Herder, 1927.

Roberti, Franciscus, *De Processibus,* 2 vols., Romae, 1926.

Savigny, *The History of Roman Law during the Middle Ages* (translated by Cathcart), Edinburgh, 1929.

Schmalzgrueber, Franciscus, *Ius Ecclesiasticum Universum,* 5 vols. in 12 tom., Romae, 1843-1845.

Schneider, Philip, *Die Entwicklung der bishöflichen Domkapitel,* Mainz, 1882.

Thomassinus, Ludovicus, *Vetus et Nova Ecclesiae Disciplina circa Beneficia et Beneficiarios,* 3 vols., Magontiaci, 1787.

Toso, A., *Ad Codicem Juris Canonici Commentaria Minora,* Città di Castella, 1921.

Vermeersch, A.,-Creusen, J., *Epitome Iuris Canonici,* 3 vols., Mechliniae: H. Dessain, vol. II, 5. ed., 1934.

Vromant, G., *Ius Missionariorum,* Vol. V, *De matrimonio,* Louvain, 1931.

Wernz, Franciscus, et Vidal, Petrus, *Ius Canonicum ad codicis normam exactum,* 7 toms., in 8 vols., Vol. II (De personis), Romae, apud aedes Universitatis Gregorianae, 1928.

Periodicals

Analecta Ecclesiastica, Paris, 1893-1911.

Apollinaris, Romae, 1928-

Canoniste Contemporain, Le, Paris, 1878-1924.

Canoniste, Le, Paris, 1925-1926.

Jus Pontificium, Romae, 1921-

Principal Articles

Boudinhon, A., "Cartophylax,"—*Le Canoniste Contemporain,* XIX (1896), 366 sq.

Couly, "Les notaires ou actuaires,"—*Le Canoniste,* XLVII (1925), 78.

Crisci, G., "Evolutio historica delegationis a iure,"—*Apollinaris,* IX (1936), 270-299.

———, "De delegation a iure in iure canonico vigenti,"—*Apollinaris,* X (1937), 513-535.

Sipos, S., "Ad officium sacrum an requiritur potestas ordinaria?"—*Jus Pontificium,* XVI (1936), 67-69.

ABBREVIATIONS

AAS—*Acta Apostolicae Sedis*
C.—*Codex Justinianus*
Can.—canon
C. Th.—*Codex Theodosianus*
Coll. Lac.—*Collectio Lacensis*
III CPB—Third Plenary Council of Baltimore (1884)
MGH—*Monumenta Germaniae Historica*
MPL—*Patrologia Latina,* Migne.
N.—*Novellae Justiniani*
R.J.—*Regula Juris*

INDEX

CANON LAW STUDIES

1. Freriks, Rev. Celestine A., C.PP.S., J.C.D., Religious Congregations in Their External Relations, 121 pp., 1916.
2. Galliher, Rev. Daniel M., O.P., J.C.D., Canonical Elections, 117 pp., 1917.
3. Borkowski, Rev. Aurelius L., O.F.M., J.C.D., De Confraternitatibus Ecclesiasticis, 136 pp., 1918.
4. Castillo, Rev. Cayo, J.C.D., Disertacion Historico-Canonica sobre la Potestad del Cabildo en Sede Vacante o Impedida del Vicario Capitular, 99 pp., 1919 (1918).
5. Kubelbeck, Rev. William J., S.T.B., J.C.D., The Sacred Pentitentiaria and Its Relation to Faculties of Ordinaries and Priests, 129 pp., 1918.
6. Petrovits, Rev. Joseph, J.C., S.T.D., J.C.D., The New Church Law on Matrimony, X-461 pp., 1919.
7. Hickey, Rev. John J., S.T.B., J.C.D., Irregularities and Simple Impediments in the New Code of Canon Law, 100 pp., 120.
8. Klekotka, Rev. Peter J., S.T.B., J.C.D., Diocesan Consultors, 179 pp., 1920.
9. Wanenmacher, Rev. Francis, J.C.D., The Evidence in Ecclesiastical Procedure Affecting the Marriage Bond, 1920 (Printed 1935).
10. Golden, Rev. Henry Francis, J.C.D., Parochial Benefices in the New Code, IV-119 pp., 1921 (Printed 1925).
11. Koudelka, Rev. Charles J., J.C.D., Pastors, Their Rights and Duties According to the New Code of Canon Law, 211 pp., 1921.
12. Melo, Rev. Antonius, O.F.M., J.C.D., De Exemptione Regularium, X-188 pp., 1921.
13. Schaaf, Rev. Valentine Theodore, O.F.M., S.T.B., J.C.D., The Cloister, X-180 pp., 1921.
14. Burke, Rev. Thomas Joseph, S.T.D., J.C.D., Competence in Ecclesiastical Tribunals, IV-117 pp., 1922.
15. Leech, Rev. George Leo, J.C.D., A Comparative Study of the Constitution, "Apostolicae Sedis" and the "Codex Juris Canonici," 179 pp., 1922.
16. Motry, Rev. Hubert Louis, S.T.D., J.C.D., Diocesan Faculties According to the Code of Canon Law, II-167 pp., 1922.
17. Murphy, Rev. George Lawrence, J.C.D., Delinquencies and Penalties in the Administration and Reception of the Sacraments, IV-121 pp., 1923.

18. O'Reilly, Rev. John Anthony, S.T.B., J.C.D., Ecclesiastical Sepulture in the New Code of Canon Law, II-129 pp., 1923.
19. Michalicka, Rev. Wenceslas Cyrill, O.S.B., J.C.D., Judicial Procedure in Dismissal of Clerical Exempt Religious, 107 pp., 1923.
20. Dargin, Rev. Edward Vincent, S.T.B., J.C.D., Reserved Cases According to the Code of Canon Law, IV-103 pp., 1924.
21. Godfrey, Rev. John A., S.T.B., J.C.D., The Right of Patronage According to the Code of Canon Law, 153 pp., 1924.
22. Hagedorn, Rev. Francis Edward, J.C.D., General Legislation on Indulgences, II-154 pp., 1924.
23. King, Rev. James Ignatius, J.C.D., The Administration of the Sacraments to Dying Non-Catholics, V-141 pp., 1924.
24. Winslow, Rev. Francis Joseph, A.F.M., J.C.D., Vicars and Prefects Apostolic, IV-149 pp., 1924.
25. Correa, Rev. Jose Servelion, S.T.L., J.C.D., La Potestad Legislativa de la Iglesia Catolica, IV-127 pp., 1925.
26. Dugan, Rev. Henry Francis, A.M., J.C.D., The Judiciary Department of the Diocesan Curia, 87 pp., 1925.
27. Keller, Rev. Charles Frederick, S.T.B., J.C.D., Mass Stipends, 167 pp., 1925.
28. Paschang, Rev. John Linus, J.C.D., The Sacramentals According to the Code of Canon Law, 129 pp., 1925.
29. Pointek, Rev. Cyrillus, O.F.M., S.T.B., J.C.D., De Indulto Exclaustrationis necnon Saecularizationis, XIII-289 pp., 1925.
30. Kearney, Rev. Richard Joseph, S.T.B., J.C.D., Sponsors at Baptism According to the Code of Canon Law, IV-127 pp., 1925.
31. Bartlett, Rev. Chester Joseph, A.M., LL.B., J.C.D., The Tenure of Parochial Property in the United States of America, V-108 pp., 1926.
32. Kilker, Rev. Adrian Jerome, J.C.D., Extreme Unction, V-425 pp., 1926.
33. McCormick, Rev. Robert Emmett, J.C.D., Confessors of Religious, VIII-266 pp., 1926.
34. Miller, Rev. Newton Thomas, J.C.D., Founded Masses According to the Code of Canon Law, VII-93 pp., 1926.
35. Roelker, Rev. Edward G., S.T.D., J.C.D., Principles of Privilege According to the Code of Canon Law, XI-166 pp., 1926.
36. Bakalarczyk, Rev. Richardus, M.I.C., J.U.D., De Novitiatu, VIII-208 pp., 1927.

37. Pizzuti, Rev. Lawrence, O.F.M., J.U.L., De Parochis Religiosis, 1927. (Not printed.)
38. Bliley, Rev. Nicholas Martin, O.S.B., J.C.D., Altars According to the Code of Canon Law, XIX-132 pp., 1927.
39. Brown, Mr. Brendan Francis, A.B., LL.M., J.U.D., The Canonical Juristic Personality with Special Reference to Its Status in the United States of America, V-212 pp., 1927.
40. Cavanaugh, Rev. William Thomas, C.P., J.U.D., The Reservation of the Blessed Sacrament, VIII-101 pp., 1927.
41. Doheny, Rev. William J., C.S.C., A.B., J.U.D., Church Property: Modes of Acquisition, X-118 pp., 1927.
42. Feldhaus, Rev. Aloysius H., C.PP.S., J.C.D., Oratories, IX-141 pp., 1927.
43. Kelly, Rev. James Patrick, A.B., J.C.D., The Jurisdiction of the Simple Confessor, X-208 pp., 1927.
44. Neuberger, Rev. Nicholas J., J.C.D., Canon 6 or the Relation of the Codex Juris Canonici to the Preceding Legislation, V-95 pp., 1927.
45. O'Keefe, Rev. Gerald Michael, J.C.D., Matrimonial Dispensations, Powers of Bishops, Priests and Confessors, VIII-232 pp., 1927.
46. Quigley, Rev. Joseph, A.M., A.B., J.C.B., Condemned Societies, 139 pp., 1927.
47. Zaplotnik, Rev. Johannes Leo, J.C.D., De Vicariis Foraneis, X-142 pp., 1927.
48. Duskie, Rev. John Aloysius, A.B., J.C.D., The Canonical Status of the Orientals in the United States, VIII-196 pp., 1928.
49. Hyland, Rev. Francis Edward, J.C.D., Excommunication, Its Nature, Historical Development and Effects, VIII-181 pp., 1928.
50. Reinmann, Rev. Gerald Joseph, O.M.C., J.C.D., The Third Order Secular of Saint Francis, 201 pp., 1928.
51. Schenk, Rev. Francis J., J.C.D., The Matrimonial Impediments of Mixed Religion and Disparity of Cult, XVI-318 pp., 1929.
52. Coady, Rev. John Joseph, S.T.D., J.U.D., A.M., The Appointment of Pastors, VIII-150 pp., 1929.
53. Kay, Rev. Thomas Henry, J.C.D., Competence in Matrimonial Procedure, VIII-164 pp., 1929.
54. Turner, Rev. Sidney Joseph, C.P., J.U.D., The Vow of Poverty, XLIX-217 pp., 1929.
55. Kearney, Rev. Raymond A., A.B., S.T.D., J.C.D., The Principles of Delegation, VII-149 pp., 1929.

56. Conran, Rev. Edward James, A.B., J.C.D., The Interdict, V-163 pp., 1930.
57. O'Neil, Rev. William H., J.C.D., Papal Rescripts of Favor, VII-218 pp., 1930.
58. Bastnagel, Rev. Clement Vincent, J.U.D., The Appointment of Parochial Adjutants and Assistants, XV-257 pp., 1930.
59. Ferry, Rev. William A., A.B., J.C.D., Stole Fees, V-135 pp., 1930.
60. Costello, Rev. John Michael, A.B., J.C.D., Domicile and Quasi-domicile, VII-201 pp., 1930.
61. Kremer, Rev. Michael Nicholas, A.B., S.T.B., J.C.D., Church Support in the United States, VI-1930.
62. Angulo, Rev. Luis, C.M., J.C.D., Legislation de la Iglesia sobre la intencion en la application de la Santa Misa, VII-104 pp., 1931.
63. Frey, Rev. Wolfgang Norbert, O.S.B., A.B., J.C.D., The Act of Religious Profession, VIII-174 pp., 1931.
64. Roberts, Rev. James Brendan, A.B., J.C.D., The Banns of Marriage, XIV-140 pp., 1931.
65. Ryder, Rev. Raymond Aloysius, A.B., J.C.D., Simony, IX-151 pp., 1931.
66. Campagna, Rev. Angelo, Ph.D., J.U.D., Il Vicario Generale del Vescovo, VII-205 pp., 1931.
67. Cox, Rev. Joseph Godfrey, A.B., J.C.D., The Administration of Seminaries, VI-124 pp., 1931.
68. Gregory, Rev. Donald J., J.U.D., The Pauline Privilege, XV-165 pp., 1931.
69. Donohue, Rev. John F., J.C.D., The Impediment of Crime, VII-110 pp., 1931.
70. Dooley, Rev. Eugene A., O.M.I., J.C.D., Church Law On Sacred Relics, IX-143 pp., 1931.
71. Orth, Rev. Raymond Clement, O.M.C., J.C.D., The Approbation of Religious Institutes, 171 pp., 1931.
72. Pernicone, Rev. Joseph M., A.B., J.C.D., The Ecclesiastical Prohibition of Books, XII-267 pp., 1932.
73. Clinton, Rev. Connell, A.B., J.C.D., The Paschal Precept, IX-108 pp., 1932.
74. Donnelly, Rev. Francis B., A.M., S.T.L., J.C.D., The Diocesan Synod, VIII-125 pp., 1932.
75. Torrente, Rev. Camilo, C.M.F., J.C.D., Las Processiones Sagradas, V-145 pp., 1932.
76. Murphy, Rev. Edwin J., C.PP.S., J.C.D., Suspension Ex Informata Conscientia, XI-122 pp., 1932.
77. Mackenzie, Rev. Eric F., A.M., S.T.L., J.C.D., The Delict of Heresy in its Commission Penalization, Absolution, VII-124 pp., 1932.

78. Lyons, Rev. Avitus E., S.T.B., J.C.D., The Collegiate Tribunal of First Instance, VI-147 pp., 1932.
79. Connolly, Rev. Thomas A., J.C.D., Appeals, XI-195 pp., 1932.
80. Sangmeister, Rev. Joseph V., A.B., J.C.D., Force and Fear as Precluding Matrimonial Consent, V-211 pp., 1932.
81. Jaeger, Rev. Leo A., A.B., J.C.D., The Administration of Vacant and Quasi-vacant Episcopal Sees in the United States, IX-229 pp., 1932.
82. Rimlinger, Rev. Herbert T., J.C.D., Error Invalidating Matrimonial Consent, VII-79 pp., 1932.
83. Barrett, Rev. John, D.M., S.S., J.C.D., A Comparative Study of the Third Plenary Council of Baltimore and the Code, IX-221 pp., 1932.
84. Carberry, Rev. John J., Ph.D., S.T.D., J.C.D., The Juridical Form of Marriage, X-177 pp., 1934.
85. Dolan, Rev. John L., A.B., J.C.D., The Defensor Vinculi, XII-157 pp., 1934.
86. Hannan, Rev. Jerome D., A.M., S.T.D., LL.B., J.C.D., The Canon Law of Wills, IX-517 pp., 1934.
87. Lemieux, Rev. Delisle A., A.M., J.C.D., The Sentence in Ecclesiastical Procedure, IX-131 pp., 1934.
88. O'Rourke, Rev. James J., A.B., J.C.D., Parish Registers, VII-109 pp., 1934.
89. Timlin, Rev. Bartholomew, O.F.M., A.M., J.C.D., Conditional Matrimonial Consent, X-381 pp., 1934.
90. Wahl, Rev. Francis X., A.B., J.C.D., The Matrimonial Impediments of Consanguinity and Affinity, VI-125 pp., 1934.
91. White, Rev. Robert J., A.B., LL.B., S.T.B., J.C.D., Canonical Ante-Nuptial Promises and the Civil Law, VI-152 pp., 1934.
92. Herrera, Rev. Antonio Parra, O.C.D., J.C.D., Legislation Ecclesiastica sobra el Ayuno y la Abstinencia, XI-191 pp., 1935.
93. Kennedy, Rev. Edwin J., J.C.D., The Special Matrimonial Process in Cases of Evident Nullity, X-165 pp., 1935.
94. Manning, Rev. John J., A.B., J.C.D., Presumption of Law in Matrimonial Procedure, XI-111 pp., 1935.
95. Moeder, Rev. John M., J.C.D., The Proper Bishop for Ordination and Dismissorial Letters, VII-135 pp., 1935.
96. O'Mara, Rev. William A., A.B., J.C.D., Canonical Causes For Matrimonial Dispensations, IX-155 pp., 1935.
97. Reilly, Rev. Peter, J.C.D., Residence of Pastors, IX-81 pp., 1935.
98. Smith, Rev. Mariner T., O.P., S.T.L., J.C.D., The Penal Law For Religious, VII-169 pp., 1935.

99. Whalen, Rev. Donald W., A.M., J.C.D., The Value of Testimonial Evidence in Matrimonial Procedure, XIII-297 pp., 1935.
100. Cleary, Rev. Joseph F., J.C.D., Canonical Limitations on the Alienation of Church Property, VIII-141 pp., 1936.
101. Glynn, Rev. John C., J.C.D., The Promoter of Justice, XX-337 pp., 1936.
102. Brennan, Rev. James H., S.S., A.M., S.T.B., J.C.D., The Simple Convalidation of Marriage, VI-135 pp., 1937.
103. Brunini, Rev. Joseph Bernard, J.C.D., The Clerical Obligations of Canons, 139 and 142, X-121 pp., 1937.
104. Connor, Rev. Maurice, A.B., J.C.D., The Administrative Removal of Pastors, VIII-159 pp., 1937.
105. Guilfoyle, Rev. Merlin Joseph, J.C.D., Custom, XI-144 pp., 1937.
106. Hughes, Rev. James Austin, A.B., A.M., J.C.D., Witnesses in Criminal Trials of Clerics, IX-140 pp., 1937.
107. Jansen, Rev. Raymond J., A.B., S.T.L., J.C.D., Canonical Provisions for Catechetical Instruction, VII-153 pp., 1937.
108. Kealy, Rev. John James, A.B., J.C.D., The Introductory Libellus in Church Court Procedure, XI-121 pp., 1937.
109. McManus, Rev. James Edward, C.SS.R., J.C.D., The Administration of Temporal Goods in Religious Institutes, XVI-196 pp., 1937.
110. Moriarity, Rev. Eugene James, J.C.D., Oaths in Ecclesiastical Courts, X-115 pp., 1937.
111. Rainer, Rev. Eligius George, C.SS.R., J.C.D., Suspension of Clerics, XVII-249 pp., 1937.
112. Reilly, Rev. Thomas F., C.SS.R., J.C.D., Visitation of Religious, VI-195 pp., 1938.
113. Moriarty, Rev. Francis E., C.SS.R., J.C.D., The Extraordinary Absolution from Censures, XV-334 pp., 1938.
114. Connolly, Rev. Nicholas P., J.C.D., The Canonical Erection of Parishes, X-132 pp., 1938.
115. Donovan, Rev. James Joseph, J.C.D., The Pastor's Obligation in Prenuptial Investigation, XII-322 pp., 1938.
116. Harrigan, Rev. Robert J., M.A., S.T.B., J.C.D., The Radical Sanation of Invalid Marriages, VIII-208 pp., 1938.
117. Boffa, Rev. Conrad Humbert, J.C.D., Canonical Provisions for Catholic Schools, X-211 pp., 1939.
118. Parsons, Rev. Anscar John, O.M., Cap., P.C.D., Canonical Elections, XII-236 pp., 1939.
119. Reilly, Rev. Edward Michael, A.B., J.C.D., The General Norms of Dispensation, X-156 pp., 1939.
120. Ryan, Rev. Gerald Aloysius, A.B., J.C.D., Principles of Episcopal Jurisdiction, XII-172 pp., 1939.

121. Burton, Rev. Francis James, C.S.C., A.B., J.C.D., A Commentary on Canon 1125, X-222 pp., 1940.
122. Miaskiewicz, Rev. Francis Sigismund, J.C.D., Supplied Jurisdiction according to Canon 209, XII-340 pp., 1940.
123. Rice, Rev. Patrick William, A.B., J.C.D., Proof of Death in Pre-nuptial Investigation, VIII-156 pp., 1940.
124. Anglin, Rev. Thomas Francis, M.S., J.C.D., The Eucharistic Fast.
125. Coleman, Rev. John Jerome, J.C.D., The Minister of Confirmation.
126. Downs, Rev. John Emmanuel, A.B., J.C.D., The Concept of Clerical Immunity.
127. Esswein, Rev. Anthony Albert, J.C.D., Extrajudicial Penal Powers of Ecclesiastical Superiors.
128. Farrell, Rev. Benjamin Francis, M.A., S.T.L., J.C.D., The Rights and Duties of the Local Ordinary Regarding Congregations of Women Religious of Pontifical Approval.
129. Feeney, Rev. Thomas John, A.B., S.T.L., J.C.D., Restitutio in Integrum.
130. Findlay, Rev. Stephen William, O.S.B., A.B., J.C.D., Canonical Norms Governing the Deposition and Degradation of Clerics.
131. Goodwine, Rev. John, A.B., S.T.L., J.C.D., The Right of the Church to Acquire Property.
132. Heston, Rev. Edward Louis, C.S.C., Ph.D., S.T.D., J.C.D., The Alienation of Church Property in the United States.
133. Hogan, Rev. James John, S.T.L., J.C.D., Judicial Advocates and Procurators.
134. Kealy, Rev. Thomas M., A.B., Litt.B., J.C.D., Dowry of Women Religious.
135. Keene, Rev. Michael James, O.S.B., J.C.D., Religious Ordinaries and Canon 198.
136. Kerin, Rev. Charles A., S.S., M.A., S.T.B., J.C.D., The Privation of Christian Burial.
137. Louis, Rev. William Francis, M.A., J.C.D., Diocesan Archives.
138. McDevitt, Rev. Gilbert Joseph, A.B., J.C.D., Legitimacy and Legitimation.
139. McDonough, Rev. Thomas Joseph, A.B., J.C.D., Apostolic Administrators.
140. Meier, Rev. Carl Anthony, A.B., J.C.D., Penal Administrative Procedure Against Negligent Pastors.
141. Schmidt, Rev. John Rogg, A.B., J.C.D., The Principles of Authentic Interpretation in Canon 17 of the Code of Canon Law.

142. Slafkosky, Rev. Andrew Leonard, A.B., J.C.D., The Canonical Episcopal Visitation of the Diocese.
143. Swoboda, Rev. Innocent Robert, O.F.M., J.C.D., Ignorance in Relation to the Imputability of Delicts.
144. Dubé, Rev. Arthur Joseph, A.B., J.C.D., The General Principles for the Reckoning of Time in Canon Law.
145. McBride, Rev. James T., A.B., J.C.D., Incardination and Excardination of Seculars.
146. Król, Rev. John J., J.C.L., The Defendant in Contentious Trials.
147. Comyns, Rev. Joseph J., C.SS.R., J.C.L., The Papal and Episcopal Administration of Church Property.
148. Barry, Rev. Garrett Francis, O.M.I, J.C.L., Violation of the Cloister.
149. Bolduc, Rev. Gatien, C.S.V., A.B., S.T.L., J.C.L., Les études dans les religions cléricales.
150. Boyle, Rev. David John, M.A., J.C.L., The Juridic Effects of Moral Certitude on Pre-Nuptial Guarantees.
151. Canavan, Rev. Walter Joseph, M.A., Litt.D., J.C.L., Profession of Faith.
152. Desrochers, Rev. Bruno, A.B., Ph.L., S.T.B., J.C.L., Le Premier Concile Plénier de Québec et le Code de Droit Canonique.
153. Dillon, Rev. Robert Edward, A.B., J.C.L., Common Law Marriage.
154. Dodwell, Rev. Edward John, Ph.D., S.T.B., J.C.L., The Time and Place for the Celebration of Marriage.
155. Donnellan, Rev. Thomas Andrew, A.B., J.C.L., The Obligation of the Missa pro Populo.
156. Eltz, Rev. Louis Anthony, A.B., J.C.L., Co-operation in Crime.
157. Gass, Rev. Sylvester Francis, M.A., J.C.L., Ecclesiastical Pensions.
158. Guiniven, Rev. John Joseph, C.SS.R., J.C.L., The Precept of Hearing Mass on Sundays and Holy Days of Obligation.
159. Gulczynski, Rev. John Theophilus, J.C.L., The Desecration and Violation of Churches.
160. Hammill, Rev. John Leo, M.A., J.C.L., The Obligations of the Traveler according to Canon 14.
161. Haydt, Rev. John Joseph, A.B., J.C.L., Reserved Benefices.
162. Huser, Rev. Roger John, O.F.M., A.B., J.C.L., The Crime of Abortion in Canon Law.
163. Kearney, Rev. Francis Patrick, A.B., S.T.L., J.C.L., The Principles of Canon 1127.

164. Linahen, Rev. Leo James, S.T.L., J.C.L., De Absolutione Complicis in Peccato Turpi.
165. McCloskey, Rev. Joseph Aloysius, A.B., J.C.L., The Subject of Ecclesiastical Law according to Canon 12.
166. O'Neill, Rev. Francis Joseph, C.SS.R., J.C.L., The Dismissal of Religious in Temporary Vows.
167. Prince, Rev. John Edward, A.B., S.T.B., J.C.L., The Diocesan Chancellor.
168. Riesner, Rev. Albert Joseph, C.SS.R., J.C.L., Apostates and Fugitives from Religious Institutes.
169. Stenger, Rev. Joseph Bernard, J.C.L., The Mortgaging of Church Property.
170. Waldron, Rev. Joseph Francis, A.B., J.C.L., The Minister of Baptism.
171. Willett, Rev. Robert Albert, J.C.L., The Probative Value of Documents in Ecclesiastical Trials.
172. Woeber, Rev. Edward Martin, M.A., J.C.L., The Interpellations.

www.ingramcontent.com/pod-product-compliance
Lightning Source LLC
LaVergne TN
LVHW050211080826
844660LV00012B/396

* 9 7 8 0 8 1 3 2 2 3 5 6 8 *